California Natural History Guides: 19

SEASHORE PLANTS

OF

SOUTHERN CALIFORNIA

BY

E. YALE DAWSON

UNIVERSITY OF CALIFORNIA PRESS

BERKELEY AND LOS ANGELES 1966

NOTE ON THE ILLUSTRATIONS

The cover illustration shows a richly-vegetated intertidal rock at Carpinteria covered with *Gigartina, Gelidium, Laminaria,* and numerous other seaweeds. I am indebted to the late Dr. H. E. Jaques for permission to reproduce a number of the line drawings from my *How to Know the Seaweeds,* published by Wm. C. Brown Co. Several of the drawings are modifications of renditions by Michael Neushul. The remainder are original or redrawings by the writer from various published sources. The color illustrations are mainly the work of Don Ollis and Dallas Clites.

UNIVERSITY OF CALIFORNIA PRESS

BERKELEY AND LOS ANGELES, CALIFORNIA

CONTENTS

Plocamium coccineum var. *pacificum*

INTRODUCTION

The southern California seashore has become one of the great playgrounds of the nation. From Gaviota Beach State Park in Santa Barbara County to the fabulous development of Mission Bay at San Diego, millions of people now visit this warm corner of our Pacific Coast every year. Marineland, Sea World, and the underwater garden of Catalina Island have given multitudes an exciting glimpse of the marine environment, while thousands more have invaded the watery world with scuba. The California shore is now a familiar place to many, and the curious plants and animals of the sea a source of widespread interest.

Unfortunately, our marine plants have received little publicity to date, and few materials are available to the layman to help him recognize and identify the many interesting and colorful kinds that he may find. This little book is intended to portray most of the common and widespread species from San Diego to Santa Barbara in a way that will make them easily identifiable without the need of microscopic equipment or the study of wordy descriptions. You will, of course, find plants that are not pictured here, but those that are presented have been selected from long experience with the marine vegetation of this coast as the ones most frequently encountered. The explanatory notes will help with some of the less common species, and the bibliography provides sources of information of more detailed nature for those who wish to take a more advanced step in marine botany.

It must be pointed out that the collection of all plant and animal specimens on the California coast is regulated by the California Department of Fish and Game, and that it is prohibited to remove any of these things from the shore without permission. Serious students and those who wish to make collections for study should obtain a collectors' permit. Others will observe, identify, and enjoy their finds, but will leave them for the next to see.

THE SOUTHERN CALIFORNIA MARINE ENVIRONMENT

The student of marine life in southern California should first become aware that, in this densely populated area of intense industrial and land development, a great many changes have taken place during the past century that have modified the characters of the plant and animal communities of the seashore. In the early 1800's the kelp beds of our coast were the home of countless playful sea otters which were slaughtered almost to extinction even before California became a state. During those early years the California Gray Whale migrated into San Diego Bay for calving season, and the Elephant Seal abounded among our islands. These phenomena of nature can never re-occur on our populated shores. There have been other changes. The extensive modification of our bays and lagoons for shipping, for marinas, and for water sports have pushed back much of the marine and marsh vegetation, although our state parks and nature preserves have held various areas in as natural a condition as possible. The kelp beds, too, have declined under the influence of pollution of many kinds and of the effects of intensive harvesting for five decades. Nevertheless, some good stands remain, and after a storm the litter of these huge marine algae on the beaches provides great interest for the inland dweller who sees them as an unfamiliar plant oddity.

Because of the widespread disturbing effects of humanity on the wildlife of the shore, the richest areas for plant and animal life are the remote and unfrequented ones. Thus, to find luxuriant growths of seaweeds unaffected by man, one must go to the Channel Islands where pollution has not taken its toll. On the mainland, the best sites for seaweed study are from Carpinteria (cover photo) to Gaviota in the north and in the vicinity of La Jolla in the south. Between these points there is much to be found, and most of the species figured in this book may be recognized, but the diversity is not so great.

Seashore plants are best observed at low tide when the light is good. Such conditions do not always occur at convenient times, for on our coast the good low tides of summer come very early in the morning, mostly before or just after sunrise. The low "minus" tides of the autumn, however, occur in the afternoon, and some of the most enjoyable field excursions can be made during our fine weather of October and November. Fortunately, good seaweeding can also be done when the tide is not low, for frequently one encounters piles of drifted seaweeds cast up on the sand from the sublittoral region. Many different species, including the colorful ones of deeper water, may be found in such drift, especially after the first fall storms, and it is both interesting and convenient to pick them out on a sunny afternoon as the tide recedes. By collecting the driftweed early and then the attached plants of a reef as the tide ebbs, one may obtain the widest selection of species common both to the intertidal and to the deeper waters. To do this, one should plan to arrive at the shore two or three hours before the predicted time of a low tide.

[7]

HOW TO COLLECT AND MOUNT
SEASHORE PLANTS

Collection and preservation of seaweed specimens is simple, and one may keep preserved material for long periods of time without mounting if a suitable container is used. It is easiest to collect specimens in plastic bags and to pickle them in a mixture of seawater and formaldehyde (about 19 parts seawater to 1 part commercial formaldehyde). If the specimens are to be kept for some time before mounting, they should be placed in a tight metal can or, if in glass, at least in a very dark place. Bleaching from light may otherwise quickly have a bad effect.

Mounting also is easy, but requires a few special materials. Specimens are prepared by spreading and pressing them onto a piece of high-quality rag paper. Regular herbarium paper may be obtained from Commercial Paper Corp., 300 Brannan Street, San Francisco. A standard plant press and drying felts should also be at hand.

The pickled seaweeds are floated out in a little tap water in a broad, white enamel pan or in a sink and the paper to be used as backing placed under them in the water. A very slight depth of water is sufficient to wet the paper and to spread and arrange the specimen on it. The paper is then withdrawn with its specimen, drained momentarily, and laid on a drying felt in the press. It may then be covered with a sheet of household waxed paper or a piece of cotton sheeting and another drying felt placed on top for the next specimen. When the pile of materials is complete, the press is strapped up and the drying allowed to proceed. The wet felts should be replaced with dry ones at least once a day until the specimens are dry. Fresh, living material may be treated in much the same way, but drying will be faster if the plants are killed and fixed in formalin before mounting.

After the specimens are dried on their backing sheets, they may be provided with appropriate labels, indicating place, date, and conditions of collecting, and mounted further on standard herbarium sheets of uniform size. Some people prefer to keep their smaller specimens in albums, but standard herbarium filing is the better long-term procedure.

Many marine algae are delicate plants whose characters can only be determined microscopically. These may often have to be preserved in liquid and prepared on microscope slides for study. For purposes of the present book, however, attention will be confined to the larger forms which may be recognized by their gross characteristics.

WHAT ARE THE SEAWEEDS?

The larger plants of the sea are almost exclusively members of a diversified assemblage known as algae. The various groups of algae include a great many small freshwater forms and marine species ranging from microscopic, unicellular ones to the giant kelps. We are concerned here with only three principal groups which include nearly all the macroscopic seaweeds, and these are known by the predominant colors which many of their members assume. Thus, we have the Green Algae (Chlorophyta) of which most members are of a distinctly green color (pl. 1, *a*; 2, *b*); the Brown Algae (Phaeophyta) of which most are of a brownish color (pl. 1, *b*; 3, *a*), including the large kelps; and the Red Algae (Rhodophyta) which are often reddish, but may also have other pigments which lend a purplish, yellowish, greenish, or brownish color (pl. 1, *c*; 2, *c*; 4, *b*; 7, *a*).

All of the algae are spore-producing plants, and the spores are microscopic. Reproductive organs, in fact, are mostly to be seen only with a microscope, but for critical identification of species they usually must be examined. Some of the reproductive structures are sufficiently conspicuous that they will be mentioned in the following pages, and the student will often find that a simple hand lens will reveal many interesting and distinctive features invisible to the naked eye.

The algae in most cases have complex life histories that include an alternation of a sexual, gamete-producing generation with a spore-producing generation. Thus, a single species may consist of three different plants, a male gametophyte plant, a female gametophyte plant, and a sporophyte plant (fig. 1). Usually these different plants resemble one another closely, but in some cases, such as the giant kelps, the sexual plants are exceedingly minute and observable only microscopically. In a few cases the sexual and the spore-producing plants are dissimilar and look like different species. In this book, only the common, conspicuous plants are presented for easy recognition.

In addition to the algae there are a few kinds of flowering plants in the sea. We have three kinds in southern California, generally referred to as "eel grass." However, both true eel grass and surf grasses occur in different habitats (see p. 79). These curious marine grasses produce true flowers and seeds.

STRUCTURE AND REPRODUCTION OF MARINE ALGAE

The macroscopic marine algae belong to three principal divisions or phyla designated by color as indicated above: Chlorophyta: Green Algae; Phaeophyta: Brown Algae; Rhodophyta: Red Algae. The colors will prove most helpful to the user of this book as a means of finding the main assemblage to which a plant belongs.

The algae have no true roots, leaves, or flowers. Although parts of many larger algae resemble roots or leaves, we treat the entire algal plant body as a *thallus*. We call the attaching portions the *holdfast*,

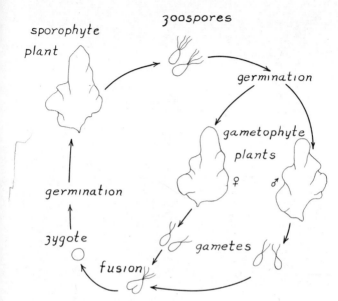

Fig. 1. Life history of *Ulva*, showing
alternation of generations.

the erect, stem-like stalk, the *stipe*. The leafy parts
are the *blades*. Some algae have finely dissected thalli
in which neither stipe nor blade can be recognized.
All have holdfasts, however, except where the plant
has broken loose and becomes free-floating for a time.
Except for a small number of Green Algae of multinucleate, non-cellular structure, the seaweeds are composed of definite cells which often have a precise and
distinctive shape and arrangement. Many of the iden-
tifying characters of the algae are to be found in the
cell structure, and there are great diversities in this
respect. Some simple forms consist of a single branched
row of cells; some of a sheet of cells in one or two
layers. Some are composed mainly of equidiametrical
cells while others have tissues made up of elongate,

[11]

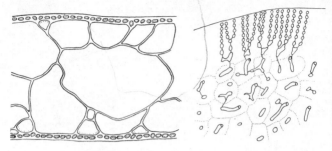

Fig. 2. Examples of cellular structure in marine algae: left, thin, definite walls of both large and small cells; right, indefinite, gelatinous walls within which the cell contents occupy small oval or elongate cavities connected by minute strands of protoplasm.

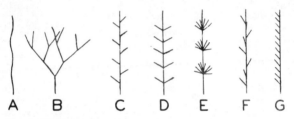

Fig. 3. Kinds of branching: A, simple (without branches); B, dichotomous; C, alternate; D, opposite; E, verticillate; F, polystichous; G, secund.

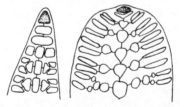

Fig. 4. Two types of growing points with apical cells.

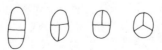

Fig. 5. Some arrangements of tetraspores in tetrasporangia: left to right, zonate, cruciate, cruciate, tetrahedral.

filamentous cells. The cell walls may be thin and definite, or sometimes very thick, gelatinous and indefinite (fig. 2).

The kind of branching of the thallus may often be distinctive and readily recognized (fig. 3). The manner of development of the thallus from terminal, basal, or lateral meristems provides special distinctive features, and the character of the apex of branches, whether with a single apical cell or a multicellular growing point, must often be determined in making identifications of genera and species (fig. 4).

The algae are all cryptogams of "hidden reproduction." They are spore producers lacking the familiar reproductive structures of flowering seed plants. The spores are of two principal kinds: motile and non-motile. In the Green and Brown algae the spores are usually motile, flagellated unicells called zoospores (fig. 1). They are produced in various ways and positions in *sporangia*. In the Red Algae the spores are all non-motile and usually are produced in groups of four *tetraspores*. These are in several distinct arrangements useful in classification (fig. 5).

As indicated above, the spores produced by the sporophyte plants usually give rise, not to more sporophyte plants, but to sexual (gametophyte) plants, often male and female. In the green and brown algae the sexual plants for the most part produce motile, flagellate gametes, often similar to the zoospores. The male and female gametes may be similar or different in size, or the female may be non-motile and fertilized by a much smaller male gamete. In the Red Algae none of the gametes is motile. The small male *spermatium* fertilizes a female gamete that does not leave the female plant, and the zygote undergoes a complex development before producing another kind of spore, called *carpospore*, which in turn reproduces the sporophyte generation (fig. 6).

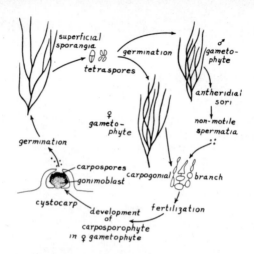

Fig. 6. Life history of the red alga, *Gracilaria*.

The examination of cellular structure and of these finer details in the algae requires the preparation of microscope slides bearing small portions of plants or cut sections which can be examined with a compound microscope. This kind of investigation may be carried out by those who wish to go beyond the scope of this introductory book. They may undertake more extensive collection and study through the use of such comprehensive literature as is listed in the bibliography on page 78.

COLOR KEY TO THE MAJOR GROUPS OF MARINE ALGAE

1. Color distinctly green (grass green, dark green, or yellowish green)...................Green Algae (Chlorophyta)
1. Color not at all distinctly green 2
   2. Color distinctly brown (dark brown to yellowish brown, but not reddish) .... Brown Algae (Phaeophytha)
   2. Color generally red or reddish, but variable, sometimes purplish or very dark, dull reddish to almost blackish, rarely greenish, occasionally brownish, but with a reddish tinge and reddish spores..Red Algae (Rhodophyta)

[14]

THE GREEN ALGAE (CHLOROPHYTA)

The members of this phylum, which includes many freshwater forms, are easily recognized by their grass-green color. Only rarely do members of other seaweed groups show a distinctly green color. Although most Chlorophyta are grass-green, a few are very dark green and some are yellowish-green.

These algae are mostly small to moderate in size, only exceptionally exceeding a foot in greatest dimension. Some are finely branched, filamentous or tufted plants; others are broad, membranous sheets. Most are intertidal species, and a few, such as *Ulva* and *Enteromorpha,* are among the most frequently encountered algae in quiet bays, harbors, and boat landings. There are not many different kinds of Green Algae to be found commonly in southern California, but some of them are exceedingly abundant.

KEY TO THE COMMON GENERA OF GREEN ALGAE IN SOUTHERN CALIFORNIA

1. Plants hollow, tubular .... *Enteromorpha*
1. Plants filamentous, cylindrical or membranous, but not tubular 2
  2. Plants thin, membranous .... *Ulva*
  2. Plants filamentous or bushy 3
3. Plants large (6 - 12 inches), dichotomously branched and spongy .... *Codium*
3. Plants smaller, filamentous, tufted 4
  4. Filaments unbranched, hair-like .... *Chaetomorpha*
  4. Filaments branched 5
5. Branched filaments without cross walls .... *Bryopsis*
5. Branched filaments septate by numerous cross walls .... *Cladophora*

Ulva (from the Celtic) Sea Lettuce

Perhaps the most striking seaweed of our intertidal rocky shores during the autumn and winter season of afternoon low tides is the very small *Ulva californica* which commonly covers rocks of the middle and upper intertidal zone with a dense, emerald green turf. The plants are only half an inch high or less, and consist of small membranous blades only two cells thick arising in large numbers from the surface of the rock.

Often growing with *U. californica*, and also scattered at lower levels, is the elongate *U. angusta* which is usually 6–10 inches long and strap-shaped. These grow in small groups or solitarily, but sometimes make an extensive community (pl. 1, *a*).

The most common *Ulva* of bays, lagoons, harbors and marshes is *U. lactuca*, a species of almost cosmopolitan distribution and of variable size and shape (fig. 7). In summer, the plant may be very expansively developed in quiet water of salt marshes and shallow bays to form large, undulate, detached sheets that at low tide are left spread on the mud.

Ulva is one of the oldest generic names among the seaweeds, having been established by Linnaeus in 1753.

Enteromorpha (intestine shape)

Enteromorpha is closely related to *Ulva* and differs mainly in being hollow. Thus, the hollow tube of *Enteromorpha* consists of a single layer of cells (fig. 8) while the membrane of *Ulva* resembles a collapsed *Enteromorpha* in which the opposing walls have become adherent to each other.

Enteromorpha is a cosmopolitan genus which may be found in almost any shallow-water marine environment. It is especially prevalent on boat hulls, buoys, docks, and woodwork (pl. 2). It is commonly associated with *Ulva* in bays and marsh waterways. It has considerable tolerance for fresh water.

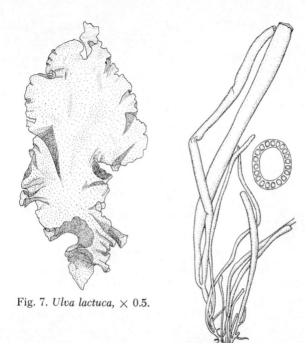

Fig. 7. *Ulva lactuca*, × 0.5.

Fig. 8. *Enteromorpha* species with basal branching, × 1, and hollow structure of a small branch, × 10.

One of the commonest species is *E. intestinalis* which is an unbranched one that arises solitarily from a small holdfast and shows a contorted and irregularly swollen character suggesting a piece of intestine.

Other common species, such as *E. compressa*, are branched, mainly at the base (fig. 8). Species recognition among these branched plants is very difficult because of exceeding variability and the fact that the really distinctive characters must be sought in the life histories rather than in external form. Some cannot be distinguished without study of the living, motile gametes and zoospores.

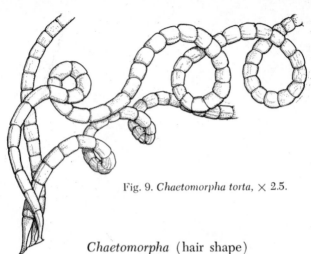

Fig. 9. *Chaetomorpha torta*, × 2.5.

Chaetomorpha (hair shape)

Chaetomorpha aerea is one of the more delicate forms of green algae in our territory, but it is sometimes exceedingly abundant in sandy places between rocks or around the edges of shallow tide pools. It resembles straight green hair. The plant consists of a single unbranched row of cells, the basal one modified for attachment. The filaments may be up to a foot long and usually grow in colonies of hundreds or thousands of individuals. Another species of less frequent occurrence but especially interesting habit is *C. torta* (fig. 9). This is ordinarily found as an epiphyte twisted and coiled around surf grass or other algae. The filaments are of much larger diameter than those of *C. aerea*, and the individual cells are visible to the naked eye.

Cladophora (branch bearing)

This is a very large genus of numerous species both in the marine and the freshwater environments. It is fairly readily recognized by its uniseriate, branched filaments in which the septa occur at rather close intervals and at the base of every branch. Most of the

Fig. 11.
Bryopsis corticulans, × 2.5.

Fig. 10. *Cladophora trichotoma,* × 25.

plants are quite delicate forms seldom reaching more than a few inches in length. They have mostly been distinguished on cell size, cell shape and branching, but some are so variable that they present considerable difficulties in classification. One of the common and distinctive ones in California is *C. trichotoma* (fig. 10) which grows at fairly high intertidal levels as a densely congested, spongy, hemispherical tuft an inch or so high and capable of holding sufficient water in the intricate network of its abundant branches that it can readily withstand lengthy periods of tidal exposure without drying out.

Bryopsis (moss-like)

This genus is one of the few in our area in which the thallus is not divided up into discrete cells. The branched axes, instead, consist of a tough, flexible cell wall forming a hollow, ramified tube filled with protoplasm that flows from one part of the plant to another.

Bryopsis corticulans is probably the commonest of several species that may be encountered along southern California. It forms dense, dark, soft clumps 2–3 inches high of numerous, delicate, pinnately-branched axes (fig. 11). It usually grows in surfy places and is our only green alga of such branching habit.

Codium (Greek, skin of an animal) Sponge Weed

This is another of the non-cellular coenocytes, but has a completely different structure from *Bryopsis*. *Codium fragile* is the most abundant species and is our most massive green alga, reaching a length of a foot or more and a weight of several pounds (fig. 12). Its texture is spongy and results from an interwoven mass of fine filaments which end at the surface in closely packed, small, bladder-like swellings, each with a sharp point. It is deep green in color, cylindrical in form and dichotomously branched. It occurs as an individual, drooping plant here and there on lower-level intertidal rocks and will not be mistaken for any other alga.

Fig. 12. *Codium fragile,* × 0.4.

There are many different kinds of *Codium* through-out warm and temperate parts of the world. Some are mat-like forms on rock surfaces, and some are hollow sponges. One in Baja California becomes rope-like and up to 25 feet long.

THE BROWN ALGAE (PHAEOPHYTA)

California is one of the few outstanding brown-algal regions in the world. Our famous beds of Giant Bladder Kelp, recently of great commercial impor-tance, extend along almost all parts of our coast and harbor a great diversity of animal life and other as-sociated plants.

Brown algae are best developed in temperate and cold waters. California has many genera and species, but the greater number occur north of Point Concep-tion. Some sixteen genera occur commonly from Santa Barbara southward, and the principal species of each of these will be taken up below. Nearly all of them are plants of fairly large size, and some are among the largest of all the algae. Most have a distinctive habit, branching, or shape, so recognition is relatively easy.

KEY TO THE COMMON GENERA OF BROWN ALGAE OF
SOUTHERN CALIFORNIA

1. Plants composed of finely branched filaments of micro-scopic dimensions . . . . *Ectocarpus*
1. Plants of larger size and more firm structure, not com-posed of free filaments of microscopic dimensions 2
   2. Plants more or less hollow throughout 3
   2. Plants not hollow throughout, although sometimes with hollow parts (air bladders) 4
3. Plants bubble-shaped, simple or convoluted . . . *Colpomenia*
3. Plants hollow-tubular, straight or contorted . . . . *Scytosiphon*
   4. Plants prostrate, crust-like 5
   4. Plants erect or drooping, not crust-like 6
5. Crust firm, more or less smooth . . . . *Ralfsia*
5. Crust soft, more or less spongy and convoluted
. . . . *Petrospongium*

Ectocarpus (external fruit)

This is a large genus of small plants. Many species of *Ectocarpus* occur as epiphytes on older, often deteriorating parts of a variety of other algae and even on animals. One curious form lives on a parasitic isopod attached to the tail of surf perch. Most are small, tufted forms less than half an inch tall, but one of the commonest species, *E. granulosus,* reaches several inches in height and grows abundantly on intertidal algae as a fine, brownish fleece. The thallus is composed of branched, uniseriate filaments which are usually terminally attenuated. The tiny dark reproductive bodies can be made out with a hand lens, but the details of these, by which many species are dis-

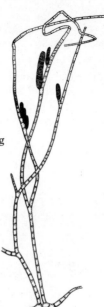

Fig. 13. *Ectocarpus* species, showing uniseriate filament and reproductive bodies, × 24.

tinguished, must be observed under high magnification (fig. 13).

Ralfsia (after British phycologist Ralfs)

In the middle and upper intertidal zone, on rocks severely and frequently exposed to sun and air, is one of the seaweeds most tolerant of desiccation. *Ralfsia* lives as a dark brown or blackish crust, often resembling tar spots so common from our submarine oil seeps. These crusts are so firmly adherent and inflexible that they cannot be removed intact from the rock, but can partly be scraped or cut off with a sharp blade. The crusts begin as more or less circular shapes, but by convergence and irregular growth may form broad expanses a foot or more across.

The tissues of *Ralfsia* are dense and the cells are extremely hygroscopic. The plants may become almost crisp dry in the sun, yet remain alive and continue growth with the first splash of the incoming tide.

There are a number of species of *Ralfsia*, but they are poorly known and the life histories for the most part are not recorded in the scientific literature. They seem to produce their fruiting bodies and motile spores and gametes mainly in winter when most investigators find it inconvenient to study algal reproduction.

Ralfsia is an encrusting plant composed of short, erect filaments which, however, are so densely packed and grown together that they form a firm, solid tissue (fig. 14).

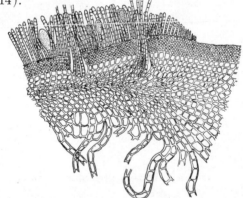

Fig. 14. *Ralfsia* species as seen in vertical section, × 58.

Petrospongium (rock sponge)

On the same severely exposed rocks in the middle intertidal zone as support crusts of *Ralfsia*, is another brown alga of prostrate habit and distinctive texture. *Petrospongium* grows as a small, adherent cushion 1–2 inches in diameter, of lobed and convoluted shape, and of a spongy, gelatinous consistency (fig. 15). It spreads less extensively than *Ralfsia*, is much thicker and can readily be removed from the rock with a dull

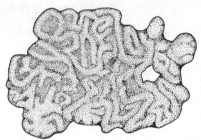

Fig. 15. *Petrospongium rugosum*, habit, × 1.

blade. The substance is soft enough that a small bit can be crushed out on a slide to reveal the structure of branched filaments in a thick jelly.

Petrospongium rugosum was originally described from Japan and subsequently found to occur on our Pacific Coast where it is now known to extend from San Francisco well into Mexico.

Pachydictyon (thick network)

The only intertidal brown algae of our region with smooth, paper-thin blades and dichotomous branching are *Pachydictyon coriaceum* (fig. 16, A) and the closely related *Dictyota flabellata*. *Pachydictyon* will be found in older collections under the name *Dictyota binghamiae*, a tooth-margined species of deep water with which it was erroneously identified. The common plant of our shores is deep brown, mostly 6–10 inches long, smooth-margined and asymmetrically dichotomous. It is an inhabitant of tide pools in the middle littoral, often associated with the similar but smaller and paler colored *Dictyota*. The two genera are distinguished only by the structure of the margins of the blades. *Dictyota* has only 3 tiers of cells throughout (fig. 16, B) while *Pachydictyon* has 5 or more along the margins.

This is another species of occurrence on both sides of the north Pacific, in California and in Japan.

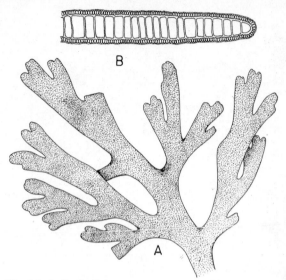

Fig. 16. A, *Pachydictyon coriaceum,* × 0.75; B, cross section of *Dictyota* species, × 24.

Zonaria (banded)

Zonaria farlowii is a handsome alga of sandy, warm tide pools at middle levels throughout southern California. The plants are densely bushy, 3–10 inches tall and attached by a spongy, felted, fibrous holdfast. It is our only benthic seaweed in which the tips of the

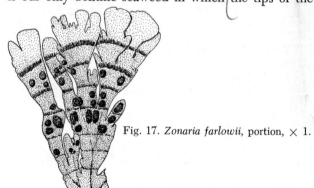

Fig. 17. *Zonaria farlowii,* portion, × 1.

growing blades appear as small fans with concentric lines (fig. 17). A related plant, *Taonia lennebackerae*, found in the same habitat, tends to be fan-shaped overall, but the blades are split and lacerated so that the character is not clearly evident.

The name, *Zonaria farlowii*, refers to the concentric zones or bands of the young blades and honors W. G. Farlow, first resident American marine botanist at Harvard University.

Dictyopteris (net wing)

Dictyopteris zonarioides is the common species of this genus in southern California. It has an interesting

Fig. 18. *Dictyopteris zonarioides*, habit, × 0.8.

distribution extending from intertidal pools to depths of 60 feet or more. The mature plants are densely, bushily branched, up to a foot high, and attached by a coarse, fibrous base growing into tough, woody older branches. The delicate, narrow, membranous blades have a distinctive midrib (fig. 18) which persists and becomes part of the woody branch system after the blade erodes away. Young, growing blades tend to be somewhat iridescent. *Dictyopteris* commonly grows in company with *Zonaria* in our region and resembles it in habit, size, and color as its name implies.

Scytosiphon (leather tube)

This is a brown alga parallel in form with the green *Enteromorpha intestinalis* and of similar size. Our *S. lomentaria* forms tubular thalli 2–12 inches long, usually gregarious in clusters from a common, crust-like attachment. Small plants are slender and straight. Large ones tend to be inflated and irregularly constricted (pl. 5). This is a very widespread plant originally described from Denmark and found on our coast from Alaska to Mexico. It is quite strictly intertidal and usually occurs in our territory as the small, slender form on very high, exposed rocks in the *Ralfsia* zone. Less frequently, larger, constricted plants are found all the way down to levels exposed only by spring tides.

Endarachne (internal spiderweb)

This is another plant of usual occurrence on high-level rocks subjected to long tidal exposure. It consists of a flat, thin blade usually an inch or less wide and 4–10 inches long, tapered at the base to a very small attachment (pl. 3). The blades often show an irregular coloration due to the production of reproductive bodies (zoospores) from more densely pigmented patches (sori) on the surface.

Endarachne was named for its characteristic dense network of fine filaments making up the internal tissue of the thallus. By this structure it can readily be distinguished from the less common *Petalonia* which resembles it superficially.

Colpomenia (sinuous membrane)

One of the most striking intertidal brown algae is a small, yellow-brown, hollow, bubble-like species known as *Colpomenia sinuosa*. This plant is widely distributed in warmer regions of the world and occurs in a variety of forms. We find it growing as colonies on rocks in open places in the middle littoral, or as an epiphyte on degenerating pieces of *Egregia* or other algae. It is usually only an inch or two in diameter and of smooth, hemispherical form. However, in summer and in warm protected areas it may become much larger, convoluted, and warty. The wall of the hollow structure is quite crisp and is usually attached very broadly to the substrate. The form and color are so distinctive that *Colpomenia* cannot be confused with any other plant in southern California (fig. 19).

Fig. 19. *Colpomenia sinuosa*, habit, × 1.

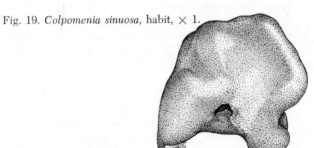

Pelagophycus (open-ocean seaweed) Elk Kelp; Bull Kelp

This alga reaches the greatest stature of any of our sea plants. *Pelagophycus porra* grows on the outer edges of the kelp beds and arises from depths of 90 feet or more. A very long, single stipe extends to the surface from a fist-size holdfast on a small rock. The top of the stipe enlarges to a large, hollow bulb 4–8 inches in diameter, and this bears a set of antler-like branches from which huge, broad, membranous blades hang down in the water like brown curtains (fig. 20). The slender stipe is often broken by storms and the blades eroded off to leave the huge antlered bulb floating far out to sea. Spanish mariners long ago were familiar with these floating objects, which they called "porra," and used them as an indication of their approach to the Mexican coast (California) on the long voyages from the Philippines. An account of the "Manila Ship" in Anson's Voyages (1748) reads as follows: ". . . and when she has run into the longitude of 96° from Cape Espiritu Santo, she generally meets with a plant floating in the sea, which being called *Porra* by the Spaniards, is, I presume, a species of sea-leek. On sight of this plant they esteem themselves sufficiently near the California shore, and immediately stand to the southward; and so much do they rely on this circumstance that on the first discovery of the plant the whole ship's company chant a solemn *Te Deum*, esteeming the difficulties and hazards of their passage to be now at an end; and they constantly correct their longitude thereby, without ever coming within sight of land."

Macrocystis (large bladder) Giant Bladder Kelp

The Pacific coast kelp beds are famous the world over. Not only are they the most extensive and elaborate submarine forests of the world, but they have provided for the greatest industrial seaweed production. So important is the harvest of kelp in California that it is regulated by the State Department of Fish and Game. Hundreds of thousands of dollars have been spent on kelp-bed maintenance and improvement. The principal product, algin, is utilized in so many industries that almost all of us use it in some way every day.

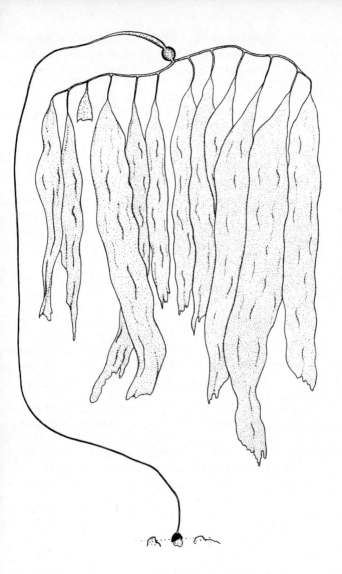

Fig. 20. *Pelagophycus porra*, habit, × 0.035.

Macrocystis is widespread in cool waters, occurring in New Zealand, Argentina, Chile, Peru, and Pacific North America, but best developed as the species *M. pyrifera* along northwestern Baja California and in the California Channel Islands. The densest bed ever measured formerly occurred along the Palos Verdes headland near Los Angeles, but metropolitan pollution some years ago wiped it out completely. Our best stands now remain in Santa Barbara and San Diego counties and in the Channel Islands.

Macrocystis is well known for its bladder-based, brown, wrinkled blades commonly found along the shore (fig. 21, B), and for its massive tangles of stipes, blades, and holdfasts that litter the beaches after a storm. The plants grow mainly in depths of 30–60 feet and form veritable forests in which the erect, entwined bundles of stipes resemble a tree trunk, and the spreading canopy of floating "stems and leaves" the crown of the tree (fig. 21, A). *Macrocystis* anchors in sand or rocks by a huge mound of root-like *haptera*, and new blade-bearing stipes grow up to the surface at extraordinarily rapid rates. Growth in length is the fastest in the plant kingdom and exceeds that of fast-growing tropical bamboos.

The massive kelp plants are all sporophytes. They produce motile zoospores from sori on special blades in lower parts of the plant. These zoospores develop into microscopic, sexual plants which rarely grow large enough to be seen with the naked eye. These delicate male and female plantlets produce sperm and eggs which, upon fertilization, recreate the large sporophyte generation. Circumstances suitable for the growth of these minute sexual plants are critical to the survival of kelp beds.

The California kelp beds were first exploited commercially during World War I as a fertilizer resource in the absence of German potash. Various chemicals were also obtained by destructive distillation, and in

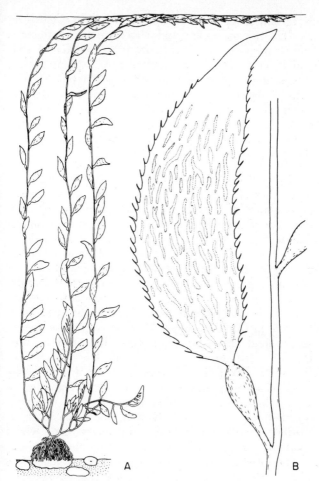

Fig. 21. *Macrocystis pyrifera*: A, habit, × 0.02; B, a blade with a basal air bladder, × 0.5.

the early 1930's the algin-extraction industry was developed. This has become by far the most important use of *Macrosystis* in this country. Algin is a hydrophilic colloidal substance very effective as àn emulsifying and suspending agent. As such it is extensively used in the ice-cream and chocolate-milk industries and in preparing a great many processed foods. It is widely employed in paints, cosmetics, pharmaceuticals, sizings, and numerous other products.

Kelp harvesting is carried out mechanically by means of a ship designed with a mowing and hauling device by which the kelp is cut several feet below the surface and drawn up into the vessel for transport to the processing plant in San Diego.

Egregia (remarkably great) Feather-Boa Kelp

Another of our large kelps that can be recognized at at glance is *Egregia laevigata,* which is unique in our area in having long, flat axes bearing numerous flat, feathery lateral blades and basal float bladders along their whole length (fig. 22). This is a kelp of shallow water, usually of surfy areas, and is one of our most abundant large algae at and just below the lowest tidal ebb. During fall and winter one often finds numerous juvenile and developmental stages of *Egregia* in the lower intertidal zone, and these appear so different from the adults that they may be mistaken as a different species. Plants less than a foot long will show a broad terminal blade from a short stipe which may or may not exhibit the beginning of lateral branches or of blades as the stipe elongates and flattens (fig. 22, C). Growth occurs in an intermediate zone at the base of the primary blade which gradually erodes away as the flat stipe elongates.

The lateral blades of young and mature vegetative plants during winter and spring are characteristically leaf-like and elongate. In many old plants during summer, however, the blades become finely dissected and hairlike, so that fragments of the two growth forms appear very different.

Fig. 22. *Egregia laevigata*: A, habit, × 0.04; B, part of the flat axis with blades and air bladders, × 0.5; C, a juvenile plant, × 0.2.

C   B

Eisenia (after naturalist Gustav Eisen) Sea Oak;
Southern Sea Palm

The famous submarine gardens of Santa Catalina
Island contain some of the finest stands of *Eisenia
arborea* and have given innumerable visitors on the

Fig. 23. *Eisenia arborea*, habit, × 0.35.

glass-bottom-boat excursions a memorable impression of marine vegetation. *Eisenia* is our most tree-like kelp, for it has an erect, woody stipe several feet long supporting a pair of branches from which the leafy blades (pl. 6) hang. Smaller, mature plants may be found intertidally in a number of our rocky shore areas (fig. 23), and juvenile specimens, which may lack conditions suitable for maturation, are often abundant. These, like young *Egregia* plants, are unlike the adults in consisting at first only of a short stipe and a broad primary blade. The young *Eisenia* blade, however, erodes away while growth proceeds from either margin of its base. As lateral blades grow out from these basal margins, which elongate and thicken, they form a pair of prong-like false branches which support the blades. This feature renders it markedly distinct from the Sea Palm (*Postelsia palmaeformis*) of surfy northern California shores.

Eisenia plants may live for a number of years and produce annual growth rings in their stipes somewhat like those of terrestrial trees.

Cystoseira (bladder chain)

Three species of *Cystoseira* occur in southern California of which *C. osmundacea* is most common. These plants are characterized by dark brown, leafy basal parts with fern-like veined "leaves." The specific name relates to a similarity to osmunda ferns. The distinctive character of the vesicles of *Cystoseira* can usually be seen only in mature plants that are at least beginning to produce their specialized reproductive branches. As these are formed the bead-like series of small, spherical vesicles appear. In *C. osmundacea* these series contain 4–10 vesicles (fig. 24, A).

Halidrys (pertaining to salt)

Juvenile and vegetative plants of *Halidrys dioica* cannot be distinguished from juveniles of the *Cystoseira* species. As soon as vesicles appear, however,

Fig. 24. A, *Cystoseira osmundacea,* habit, × 0.38; B, *Sargassum palmeri,* dissected leaf and vesicle, × 0.75; C, *Sargassum agardhianum,* leaf and vesicle, × 1.4; D, *Halidrys dioica,* flattened vesicle series, × 0.38.

they may be recognized at a glance, for the series of vesicles of *Halidrys* are flattened instead of spherical and bead-like (fig. 24, D). Both *Halidrys* and *Cystoseira* are common plants of lower littoral tide pools and of shallow subtidal waters where they may reach several feet in length. They have been growing along southern California for a long time, for in the Doheny Palisades near San Juan Capistrano and in other Miocene diatomite and siltstone shales of this region, fossil specimens of *Halidrys* and *Cystoseira* are common and show only minor evolutionary variation from present-day plants.

Although *Halidrys* is old and may once have been widespread, it survives today only in California and in Atlantic Europe.

Sargassum (from Portuguese *sarga*, a kind of grape)

Portuguese mariners of the fifteenth century named the Sargasso Sea, that vast Atlantic eddy filled with drifting seaweed buoyed up by their small, grape-shaped air vesicles. We now give these plants the name *Sargassum*, representing a genus of brown algae of wide tropical and subtropical distribution. We have two kinds in warmer areas of southern California, of quite different vegetative characters, but readily recognized by their solitary little air vesicles scattered through the branched and bushy thalli. *S. palmeri* is the common one at Catalina Island (fig. 24, B) and *S. agardhianum* (fig. 24, C) in San Diego County and in warm spots and pools northward to Point Dume.

Pelvetia (after French botanist, Pelvet)

The intertidal marine climate of southern California is too warm and dry for the common rockweeds of the northern hemisphere known as *Fucus*. Instead, we have the genus *Pelvetia* and a similar one, *Hesperophycus*, whose members occupy the tops of rocks in exposed, upper intertidal situations. *Pelvetia fastigiata* is an olive-greenish-brown plant about a foot long when well developed, and of drooping habit. The thick, narrow branches are dichotomous, and mature, fertile plants have swollen branch tips from which the reproductive bodies are extruded from numerous pores. *Hesperophycus harveyanus* (fig. 25) occupies similar or even drier intertidal areas than *Pelvetia* and is distinguished by a fairly distinct midrib bordered on either side by a row of white hair spots. These two plants are the only moderately large, branched algae at high levels in our region. A distinctive slender and finely-branched form of *Pelvetia fastigiata* occurs at Catalina Island.

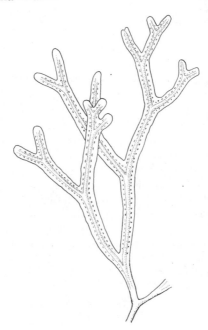

Fig. 25. *Hesperophycus harveyanus*, × 1.

THE RED ALGAE (Rhodophyta)

The Red Algae are the most abundant seaweeds of the world. There are more than 4000 species, and they occur in almost every conceivable marine habitat from the highest intertidal levels to the lowermost limits of light, but very few live in fresh or brackish water. Almost all grow attached to rocks or to other algae. None live in the floating state as does *Sargassum*.

The Red Algae do not grow as large as some of the brown kelps, but a few reach lengths of 8–10 feet. Some of the species, especially epiphytic ones, are quite small, but almost always they are visible to the naked eye. In tropical seas the Rhodophyta tend to be mostly small forms, but in temperate waters, such as ours, the average size is from 2 to 10 inches.

One of the most interesting features of the Red Algae is their color. Although they contain green chlorophyll, that pigment is generally masked by other pigments, especially the red phycoerythrin. In brightly lighted intertidal habitats the pigments are often so dense and so mixed that a dark purplish, olive, brownish or blackish color is observed, and the beginner in phycology often confuses some of the dark-pigmented red algae with brown algae. In well-shaded places or in deeper waters, the red pigments are dominant, and the plants are almost invariably pink or red. This red color represents a specific adaptation of the plants to growth in the dim and limited light of deep water, for water absorbs red, orange, and yellow light very quickly and allows only the green and blue to penetrate to depth. The red pigment is able to absorb and use these deeply penetrating rays which are not available to other colors of algae, and they permit some Rhodophyta to live at depths as great as 600 feet.

[41]

A great majority of red seaweeds have a complex life history that includes not one, but three different plants. Thus, unlike the Brown Algae, in which the one conspicuous plant in the life history is usually the sporophyte, the red algae have, in addition to the sporophyte, a male and a female plant, and all of these are similar in size and appearance (fig. 6). This circumstance provides for many complexities in classification, for a critical identification of a given species may require the presence of the male, the female, and the spore-producing phases. In some species one can recognize the different phases easily, but in most cases microscopic examination is necessary. Female plants are most readily distinguished, for the masses of carpospores produced after sexual fertilization are visible as dark spots, lumps, or papillae in or on the thallus and are generally referred to as *cystocarps* (fig. 26).

Sporophyte plants are most commonly encountered in a majority of species. They usually bear tetraspores. These are often produced on specialized branches or bladelets or in visible patches (sori) on the thallus.

Male plants are usually the least frequent, and their minute spermatia can be seen only under high magnification.

In the following treatment, reproductive characters will be used only where they are readily observed with no more equipment than a hand lens. Although in a local flora such as this the larger and commoner plants can be identified with relative ease, one should realize that, since many less common forms are not treated, and since exceeding variability occurs among many common ones, he cannot expect every specimen to fit either a key or an illustration. When difficulties are encountered, one should turn to one of the more comprehensive treatises listed in the bibliography.

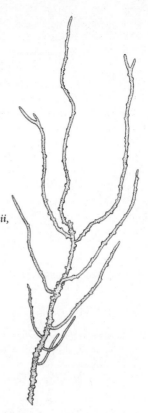

Fig. 26. *Gracilariopsis sjoestedtii,* showing prominent, superficial cystocarps on the cylindrical branches, × 1.

Key to the Common Genera of Red Algae of Southern California

[43]

6. Plants epiphytic as thin, delicate crusts ...... *Melobesia*
6. Plants larger, forming stony masses on rocks ....
.... *Lithophyllum* (or *Lithothamnium*)
7. Plants forming a thin red film on rocks ..... *Hildenbrandia*
7. Plants not forming film-like crusts 8
   8. Plants membranous or leafy, the blades 20 times or
     more as broad as thick 9
   8. Plants cylindrical, compressed or flattened, but not
     membranous or leafy 20
9. Plants occurring as numerous small blades ½ inch long
or less on surf grass .... *Smithora*
9. Plants larger, saxicolous or epiphytic, but not on surf
grass 10
   10. Plants usually epiphytic (sometimes on rocks) 11
   10. Plants strictly on rocks (or found in drift) 13
11. Blades bearing small hooks; strictly epiphytic...*Acrosorium*
11. Blades without small hooks; not always epiphytic 12
   12. Blades usually with very small marginal leaflets;
     delicate veins usually evident, at least with a hand
     lens .... *Cryptopleura*
   12. Blades usually more or less fan-shaped and divided
     into many segments; without veins or marginal leaf-
     lets .... *Callophyllis*
13. Blades with small marginal teeth 14
13. Blades with smooth margins, marginal papillae, or leaflets, but not toothed 15
   14. Plants about 1 inch tall, usually simple, under surf
     grass .... *Anisocladella*
   14. Plants larger, branched, under low-level overhangs
     or in drift .... *Nienburgia*
15. Blades with anastomosing veins .... *Polyneura*
15. Blades without anastomosing veins 16
   16. Blades ruffled but not branched .... *Porphyra*
   16. Blades more or less branched 17
17. Blades with superficial and marginal papillae or with
small marginal leaflets .... *Gigartina*, in part
(*G. armata*, *G. spinosa*, *G. volans*)
17. Blades with smooth margins 18
   18. Plants red or reddish 19
   18. Plants purplish or dark colored .... *Rhodoglossum*
19. Blades bright reddish, broadly fan-shaped, very thin but
stiff; usually less than 3 inches high .... *Rhodymenia*
19. Blades dull reddish to brownish, not so distinctly fan-
shaped, rather thick and fleshy, usually over 5 inches
high .... *Gracilaria textorii* v. *cunninghamii*

[44]

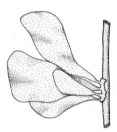

Fig. 27. *Smithora naiadum* on a leaf of *Phyllospadix,* × 5.

Smithora (after American phycologist G. M. Smith)

Although our abundant intertidal surf grass is usually an emerald green, from time to time it takes on a mottled purplish color, and close examination reveals that it is covered with a small epiphytic alga. *Smithora naiadum* (fig. 27) is an obligate epiphyte on *Phyllospadix* on whose leaves it forms abundant tiny purplish, membranous blades that arise from small fleshy cushions. It was formerly thought to represent a small species of *Porphyra*, but as the life history was worked out, it proved to have a distinctive and complex reproductive cycle. It is seasonal and periodic. Sometimes only the tiny reddish cushions will be observed dotting the leaves which commonly also bear the minute crusts of *Melobesia*.

Porphyra (purple) Laver; Nori

Porphyra perforata is a red alga of extremely hygroscopic character. It is a membranous, ruffled blade without stipe, of deep, purplish color (pl. 7), and occurs usually on rocks at very high levels in the *Ralfsia* and *Pelvetia* zone. It is seasonal and is best developed in our territory during late winter and spring. It has a gelatinous, almost rubbery texture when partially dehydrated, and is frequently collected by oriental Americans as a foodstuff known as nori. The Japanese nori, indeed, is the most extensively cultivated seaweed of the world and provides for an enormous marine agricultural industry involving more than 400,000 workers.

P. perforata is one of numerous species of the genus, many of which are grown as nori in Japan under a unique cultural procedure. The nori grounds are broad, shallow, muddy bays. At low tide during autumn, millions of bamboo poles are driven into the mud and miles of coarse-mesh nets strung on them in such a way that they are exposed at low tide. *Porphyra* spores germinate on the netting and grow into harvestable plants in a few months. Harvesting is done by hand from a narrow, one-man boat that moves up and down the net lines. The nori is pulled off, dumped into a basket, collected by a mother boat and returned to the processing yards where it is chopped into fragments and spread on small mats to dry. The dry nori is removed as a thin sheet, folded or cut and packaged for market. It is consumed in large quantities as an additive in a multitude of oriental dishes. In recent times, up to 2½ billion dried sheets have been produced in a single year.

A few years ago it was discovered that *Porphyra* (which is a sexual plant) has an alternation of generations in which the sporophyte plants are minute, filamentous forms that live in the calcareous substance of sea shells. These small plants formerly were known under the genus name *Conchocelis*. The conchocelis stage of *Porphyra* is now grown commercially in oyster shells and used in "seeding" the nori plantation waters. The English botanist, Dr. Kathleen Drew Baker, who worked out this unusual algal life history, is commemorated by a monument on Tokyo Bay.

Gelidium (from *gelu*, frost; gelatin) Agarweed

The novice will find *Gelidium* one of the puzzling genera in the range of size among several of its common members. Distinctive characters, however, in the tough, cartilaginous texture and the slender, compressed form of the branches may be learned quickly, and there are some microscopic characters which make the genus easy to identify (single apical cell; minute, wire-like filaments in the medulla).

In southern California a widely prevalent species in the middle littoral zone is *Gelidium coulteri*. This is a small, densely tufted plant 1–2 inches tall of distichous-pinnate branching, the ultimate pinnae tending to be prong-like. Lower down, in pools and at mean lower low water and below, other, larger species of *Gelidium* occur of which *G. purpurascens* and *G. cartilagineum* are the most frequent (pl. 7). A distinctive character of these latter is found in the young branchlets which are geniculate at first (as an arm bent at the elbow).

G. cartilagineum is our largest *Gelidium,* reaching a size of 3 feet and occurring in sufficient abundance to have commercial significance. It is one of the very best species from which to extract agar, and was extensively harvested by diver along southern California during World War II when Japanese agar supplies were cut off. Raw *Gelidium* for agar manufacture is now collected mainly in Baja California by cheap labor. Japan is still the major refiner and exporter of finished agar which is used in many food and pharmaceutical industries and particularly in the making of culture media for microbiological laboratories.

Pterocladia (wing branch)

This genus is very closely related to *Gelidium* and is technically distinguished mainly by the cystocarps having only one pore instead of two. Female plants, however, are infrequently found, so other means of identification are better used. Our one common species, *P. pyramidale* (pl. 6). is abundant in the middle and lower littoral zone, in and around tide pools as a densely bushy, finely branched, dull purplish plant 4–6 inches high. The branching is two-ranked in one plane and the parts are much flatter and thinner than those of *Gelidium.* Older plants show attenuation of the ultimate branchlets which become congested and tangled.

Pterocladia is also useful in agar manufacture, but is harvested for this purpose mainly in New Zealand and Australia.

Leptocladia (delicate branch)

Leptocladia binghamiae (pl. 8) is an example of one of the algae of deeper waters that may be encountered in beach drift, especially after a storm. Mrs. Bingham, an amateur algal collector of Santa Barbara, made the first herbarium specimens of this plant some time during the 1880's. She sent examples to J. G. Agardh in Sweden where the plant was named. This alga is usually 15–30 cm. high and repeatedly, irregularly, alternately branched in 4 to 5 orders, with the branches lying in one plane. It is best recognized by microscopic examination of a cross section of the thallus which reveals a single large central cell representing a prominent axial filament in the medulla of this species.

Hildenbrandia (after Austrian botanist Hildenbrand)

Smooth stones and eroded shells from the bottom of tide pools often exhibit what appear to be deep red stains or paint spots on the surface. These red blotches are the thin, adherent films of the non-calcareous, crustose red alga *Hildenbrandia prototypus.* It is a cosmopolitan plant, and once one is familiar with it, he will notice it on rocks almost everywhere, from the walls of sea caves and the sides of intertidal boulders to rock and shell surfaces from considerable depths. The crusts are so thin and firm that a sharp blade is required to remove even a tiny scraping. A hand lens will reveal the minute pits in the crust (conceptacles) which contain the tetrasporangia. Specimens of *Hildenbrandia*, like *Ralfsia*, are best collected on pieces of the substrate they inhabit.

Corallina (small coral)

This is our most widespread and prevalent jointed calcareous alga (pl. 1, c). The genus is readily recognized by its pinnate branching (fig. 28), which is usually more or less distichous, and by its reproductive conceptacles which are terminal on the segments. The plant is provided flexibility against wave shock by the minute uncalcified pads between the stony segments.

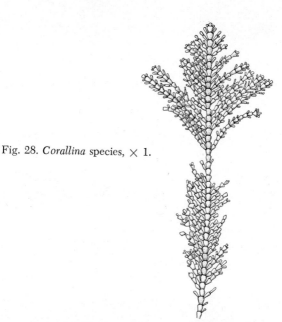

Fig. 28. *Corallina* species, × 1.

One of the commonest of all intertidal algae in southern California is *Corallina vancouveriensis* which forms dense tufts and mats through the middle and lower littoral zones. It occurs in a variety of forms which tolerate a wide range of environmental conditions from the Aleutian Islands to Mexico.

A large species of tide pools and the sublittoral is *C. officinalis* var. *chilensis*. This is the medicinal corallina of the ancients, named by Linnaeus for its favored use as a vermifuge during many centuries prior to 1775.

Bossiella (after Dutch phycologist Madam Weber van Bosse)

Our common species of *Bossiella* are distinguished from *Corallina* by their calcified segments, which have a peculiar wing-nut shape, and by the conceptacles

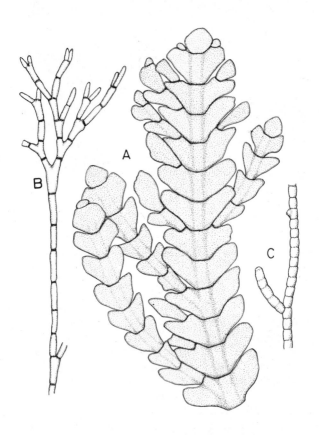

Fig. 29. A, *Bossiella insularis*, showing wing-nut-shapped calcified segments of upper part of a main branch, × 4.5; B, *Jania tenella*, × 18; C, *Lithothrix aspergillum*, part of a branch with a conceptacle, × 5.

being borne on the faces of these flat segments. *B. dichotoma* is our most prevalent intertidal species, but in the sublittoral zone *B. orbigniana* occurs commonly and is cast up in drift. Both are dichotomously branched species, but others, such as *B. insularis*, are pinnately branched (fig. 29, A).

Some species of *Bossiella* and of *Corallina* are remarkably tolerant of pollution. Much of the rocky shore area in the vicinity of Los Angeles is more or less polluted by metropolitan wastes, and during the past half century the proportion of articulated coralline algae has risen prominently. Some can grow in close proximity to sewer outfalls such as those bossiellas on the Port Hueneme breakwater which are attached and living within 20 feet of the outfall "boil."

Lithothrix (stone hair)

This genus contains the single species *Lithothrix aspergillum* which is a common tide-pool inhabitant in our area. It is finely branched, tufted, and resembles a coarse shock of bristles. The slender branches, less than a millimeter thick, are composed of a great many minute, stony segments only about as long as wide, and these bear lateral conceptacles (fig. 29, C).

Although originally described from Vancouver Island in 1867, this plant shows its most abundant growth along the warm shores of southern California.

Male, female, and asexual plants of the various jointed corallines are so similar that one must usually look at the contents of the conceptacles for tetraspores, carpospores, or spermatia in order to distinguish the three different plants of the life history.

Jania (one of the mythical sea nymphs)

This is a genus of tropical jointed corallines that reaches into California only in local warm spots. The commonest species is *Jania natalensis*, a plant of peculiar distribution in South Africa, South Australia, and California. It occurs here as small tufts and clusters in warm tide pools from La Jolla to Lechuza Point north of Point Dume. It is recognized by its slender, cylindrical, dichotomous branches of gray-pink color, 1–2 inches tall. Another species of much more delicate proportions and usually of epiphytic habit, *J. tenella* (fig. 29, B), occurs in San Diego County and at Catalina Island.

Melobesia (one of the mythical sea nymphs)

Melobesia mediocris is our smallest calcareous, crustose coralline alga, but one which can be identified with ease simply because it is an obligate epiphyte on surf grass. It forms tiny whitish crusts only as wide as the *Phyllospadix leaf* (fig. 30) and causes such infected leaves to sparkle with these glistening light spots in sunlit water. Most of the species and genera of these smaller crustose corallines must be studied carefully to distinguish them. A hand lens will reveal the small, mound-like reproductive conceptacles on the surface of the rounded crusts.

Lithophyllum (stone leaf); *Lithothamnium*
(stone branch) The Nullipores

The most widespread of all the marine algae are the rock-inhabiting, crustose corallines of the genera *Lithophyllum* and *Lithothamnium*. Plants of one or the other of these genera occur from the high Arctic and Antarctic through the tropics, from Greenland fjords to Caribbean reefs, from intertidal pools to the uttermost limits of light at depths of up to 500 feet. They may grow as a thin, calcareous film only a few cells thick, or as thick, knobby, stony masses widely spreading on rocks and several inches thick. They are not especially prominent in southern California, but several species occur of which *Lithothamnium giganteum* (fig. 31) is one of the larger nodular ones.

The genera and species of crustose corallines can

Fig. 30. *Melobesia mediocris*, epiphytic on *Phyllospadix*,
× 1.15.

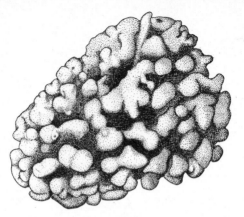

Fig. 31. *Lithothamnium giganteum,* × 1.2.

satisfactorily be identified only by close microscopic examination, and there are only a bare handful of specialists in the world who profess to know this difficult group at all well.

Closely related to *Lithophyllum* and *Lithothamnium* is the strictly tropical genus *Porolithon* to which great importance is attached because of its major role in the amazing biological and geological phenomenon of the coral reef. Coral reefs might better be known as algal reefs, for a majority of them are composed predominantly of calcareous algae. *Porolithon,* in fact, is the principal cementing and binding agent in such reefs and provides for the growth and control of the reef margin. Drill holes thousands of feet deep show that fossil calcareous algal material continues all the way to bedrock.

Prionitis (glistening)

This genus includes several species that characteristically occur in surfy places within our area at about mean low tide level and below, or in deep tide pools. They are coarse plants of narrow, compressed branches, often 2 feet long, of deep, dull purplish-red color and almost cartilaginous texture. The commonest one, *P. lanceolata*, is pinnately branched, but *P. cornea* is primarily dichotomous (fig. 32). Perhaps the most characteristic feature of nearly all species is the presence of irregular series of very short, determinate, pinnate branchlets along the main axes. The internal structure is of densely packed filamentous cells. The cystocarps are deeply embedded and do not project on the surface.

Callophyllis (beautiful leaf)

Befitting the name, these plants are among the most brilliantly colored and attractively branched of our seaweeds. They are usually found in deep waters in which the red phycoerythrin pigment is prominently developed. They are plants of driftweed, and may be sought best after the first winter storms. They are mostly flat, thin-bladed species of roughly fan-shaped

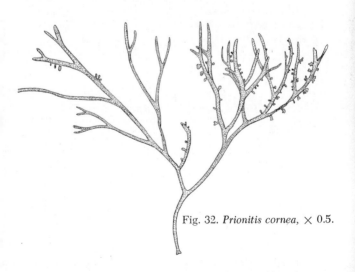

Fig. 32. *Prionitis cornea*, × 0.5.

outline, although they are often finely dissected. *C. flabellulata* is a common one recognized by its emergent cystocarps which tend to be arranged around the margins of the blades (fig. 33). *C. violacea* is a narrow species with longer segments (pl. 6). It is a common epiphyte on larger sublittoral algae in southern California and has a very narrowly and finely branched subspecies.

Callophyllis may be recognized by its cross-sectional structure which is unique among our flat red algae in having small, angular cells scattered among large, parenchymatous cells (fig. 33, B).

Agardhiella (after Swedish phycologist J. G. Agardh)

Agardhiella tenera is a widespread species along Pacific America from Canada to the Galapagos Islands. The coarser, northern forms were until recently considered to be a separate species, *A. coulteri*. We find the plant as an occasional intertidal, tide-pool, or subtidal species. Cystocarpic plants are easiest to identify. These have slender, long, fleshy cylindrical branches with few lateral branchlets and embedded cystocarps which form bulges on the surface. Sterile

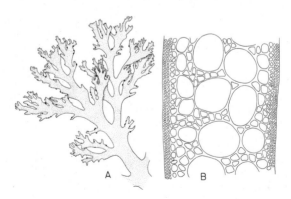

Fig. 33. *Callophyllis flabellulata*: A, habit, × 1; B, cross-sectional structure, × 120.

plants resemble *Gracilariopsis* (see fig. 26), but they are readily separated when a cross section is examined, for *Agardhiella* has a central core of fine filamentous cells within the medulla (fig. 34).

J. G. Agardh and his father C. A. Agardh were the leading European phycologists in Sweden throughout the nineteenth century. Many of our California seaweeds were described by the younger Agardh from collections made around Santa Barbara in about 1880.

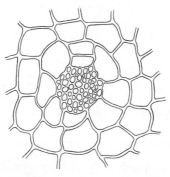

Fig. 34. *Agardhiella tenera*. Inner medulla as seen in cross section, showing central core of cells of small diameter, × 150.

Plocamium (braided hair)

The most attractive of our common seaweeds, both in color and in lacy form, is *Plocamium coccineum* var. *pacificum* (pl. 8), abundant in tide pools and on down to considerable depths. It is easily recognized by its bright red color, and distichous, sympodial branching which is a succession of zig-zags as each main axis is displaced to the side by the next branch which momentarily becomes the main axis (see p. 4). In addition to the common red species is the smaller *P. violaceum* of more purplish color and with incurved rather than somewhat recurved branchlets.

Plocamium makes very fine dry preparations when pressed on white paper. It has long been used as a colorful decoration for greeting cards.

Gracilaria (slender or delicate)

The slender, stringy, cylindrical *Gracilaria verrucosa* (*G. confervoides*) is the most widely distributed of the gracilarias, but is an exception in the genus. Nearly all of the other species are flat forms. *G. verrucosa* is identical in vegetative structure and form with species of *Gracilariopsis* (see fig. 26), but our common, flat *Gracilaria textorii* var. *cunninghamii* (fig. 35) is distinct from our other algae by its narrow-angled dichotomous branching, relatively large size (6–12 inches) and parenchymatous structure. It is usually deep, dull reddish, fleshy in texture and inhabits intertidal pools and the sublittoral zone (fig. 35).

The species, *G. textorii*, has various subspecies in the Gulf of California and also in Japan.

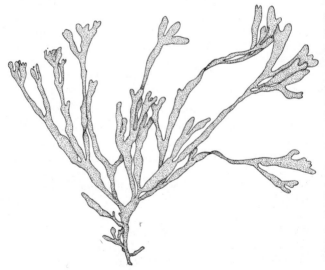

Fig. 35. *Gracilaria textorii* var. *cunninghamii*, habit, × 0.5.

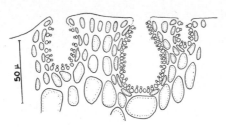

Fig. 36. *Gracilariopsis andersonii*, showing spermatangial cavities in cross-sectional view of a branch.

Species of *Gracilaria* and *Gracilariopsis* are agarphytes second only to *Gelidium* in commercial importance. Various species are used in different parts of the world. *Gracilaria verrucosa* often occurs abundantly in sheltered bays such as lower San Diego Bay where, during World War II, it was collected commercially for a short time.

Gracilariopsis (related to *Gracilaria*)

Unlike the majority of *Gracilaria* species, all *Gracilariopsis* are cylindrical. We have two common kinds. *G. andersonii* is a densely branched, reddish plant that grows almost invariably on stones partially embedded in sand. The plant withstands partial sand burial and grows up through to form tufts 4–10 inches tall in middle littoral flats and pools. The tufts tend to be corymbose. Male plants are distinctive in their sac-like spermatangial cavities, but these must be seen under high magnification (fig. 36).

An equally common species is *G. sjoestedtii* (fig. 26) which resembles *Gracilaria verrucosa* except in reproductive details. It is, however, the most common of our algae of slender, stringy form in the southern California intertidal region. The strongly emergent, hemispherical cystocarps distinguish it from slender forms of *Agardhiella*, as does also the strictly parenchymatous medulla.

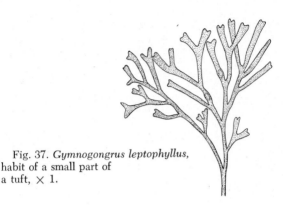

Fig. 37. *Gymnogongrus leptophyllus*,
habit of a small part of
a tuft, × 1.

Gymnogongrus (naked swelling)

This is a small genus of flattened plants of regular
dichotomous branching and of dense, but parenchymatous structure. Our commonest species is the smallest one, *G. leptophyllus* (fig. 37) which forms tufts
2 to 3 inches tall in lower littoral pools. The plants
consist of erect axes which are at first cylindrical, attached by a thin, spreading, discoid holdfast, and then
flattened, but narrow and more or less divaricately but
densely dichotomously branched. The segments become progressively shorter in upper parts and tend
to be somewhat matted or entangled.

Gigartina (grapestone)

The several common members of this genus are
often the most prevalent and conspicuous algae in the
lower intertidal zone. Two of the most abundant species, *G. canaliculata* (fig. 38) and *G. leptorhynchos*,
don't look at all like red algae insofar as color is con-

cerned, for both are very dark purplish to almost black, due to exceedingly dense pigments. Reddish coloration can be detected in younger parts, in thin sections, or by examining the spores. *G. canaliculata* is especially important as the commonest rock-cover alga in exposed middle and lower intertidal surfy areas (front cover photo). It is an abundantly and narrowly branched plant only 3–4 inches tall with dense, spinulose, determinate branchlets in upper parts. Its morphology is the most divergent of any member of the genus in our area.

Most gigartinas are quite distinctly and broadly flattended and are easily recognized by the multitude of minute papillae or prong-like structures covering the

Fig. 38. *Gigartina canaliculata,* habit, × 1.

surfaces of the blades. In the large, blade-like species, these are especially conspicuous (pl. 5; pl. 6) and render the plants easily identified. In the blackish, rather narrow *G. leptorhynchos*, in which the papillae are elongate and soft, one must look carefully to recognize resemblances to the broad, red species. A cross section, however, reveals that all of these have a similar structure of fine filaments running through a thick jelly.

Gigartina is a genus of temperate waters and reaches some of the largest sizes for red algae. A Tasmanian species (*G. gigantea*) may attain a length of 5 feet and a breadth of over 2 feet. Our larger, broader species are usually found in deep water, but are cast up as drift. Some of intermediate size, however, such as *G. armata* and *G. spinosa* (pl. 6) are commonly encountered in lowermost tideways and pools.

Rhodoglossum (red tongue)

Our only common species of this genus, *Rhodoglossum affine*, is, despite the Latin name, hardly to be compared with a red tongue. It is a dull, reddish-brown or purplish, flat, dichotomously branched plant 3–4 inches tall (pl. 4). It occupies the same exposed-rock habitat as *Gigartina canaliculata* and mingles with it. *Rhodoglossum* is closely related to *Gigartina*, but has smooth blades without any superficial papillae or outgrowths. It has a similar internal structure, but the cystocarps and tetrasporangia are embedded.

Very closely related to *Rhodoglossum affine*, also, is the Atlantic *Chondrus crispus*, world famous as Irish Moss and the basis of a great seaweed industry. Irish Moss was originally a product of Europe used in making a kind of milk pudding, but in recent decades has yielded the valuable vegetable-gelatin extract, carrageenin. For this phycocolloid, large quantities of *Chondrus* are harvested in New England and the maritime provinces of Canada. Its use is mainly as industrial stabilizers and emulsifiers.

a. A green-algal habitat of *Ulva* and *Enteromorpha* at Ventura.

b. A brown-algal habitat of *Egregia* at Santa Barbara.

c. A red-algal habitat of dark *Gigartina* and pink *Corallina* at La Jolla.

Plate 1

a. A sea-grass habitat at Loon Point, Santa Barbara County, with the surf-grass *Phyllospadix*.

Plate 2

b. The red alga *Acrosorium uncinatum*.

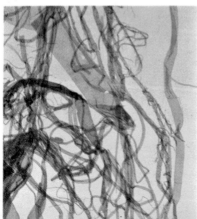

c. Green algae —two species of *Enteromorpha*.

Plate 3   a. *Endarachne binghamiae.*

b. *Nienburgia andersoniana.*

Plate 4

a. *Polyneura
latissima.*

b. *Rhodoglossum
affine.*

Plate 5

a. *Scytosiphon lomentaria.*

b. *Gigartina harveyana.*

a. *Eisenia arborea* blades; *Gigartina spinosa.*

Plate 6

c. *Pterocladia pyramidale.*

b. *Callophyllis violacea.*

*Porphyra
perforata.*

*Gelidium
purpurascens.*

*Phyllophora
clevelandii.*

a. *Plocamium coccineum* var. *pacificum*.

Plate 8

b. *Leptocladia binghamiae*.

Gastroclonium (hollow branch)

This is a genus identified with ease by means of its ultimate branchlets being hollow and provided with diaphragms to form a series of small chambers (fig. 39). However, in southern California our plants of *G. coulteri* tend to bear rather few of these hollow branchlets and to consist largely of cylindrical, fleshy, branched stipe parts. Furthermore, the tender hollow parts seem to be attractive food for invertebrates and commonly to be eaten off to the solid stipe. Accordingly, one must look for well-developed specimens not suffering from foraging in order to make satisfactory identification. Plants up to 10 inches long will be found in pools or on the sides of rocks not severely exposed in the lower intertidal zone. A closely related genus, *Coeloseira*, with these chambered branchlets, may also be found. It looks like a diminutive edition of *Gastroclonium* only 1 inch high or less.

Rhodymenia (red membrane)

Color in *Rhodymenia* is true to its name. Always pink or red, these small, dichotomously branched, digitate or fan-shaped blades are commonly found at

Fig. 39. *Gastroclonium coulteri*, branch portion, × 1.5.

lowest tide levels under overhanging rocks or in clefts and crevices where the light is subdued and there is limited exposure to air. There are two common species. *R. californica* looks like a small edition of the larger, *R. pacifica*, which reaches three to five inches. Both species range down into the sublittoral to moderate depths of 20 to 30 feet, but do not extend to the dim regions inhabited by the superficially similar *Phyllophora clevelandii* (pl. 7). This latter plant is one of our seaweeds strictly limited to deep water at 80 to 150 feet.

Rhodymenia has a strictly parenchymatous structure. Another distinctive feature of our two common species is the presence of spreading stolons from the base of the stipe. The blade segments are rounded and the margins smooth.

Ceramium (pitcher)

Among our delicate forms of marine algae is a large genus of small, dichotomous plants of cylindrical form. The ceramiums are often epiphytic, but some are tufted forms on rocks. They seldom are more than 2 to 3 inches tall. *C. eatonianum* is a very common one in southern California intertidal waters. It is densely tufted, dark purplish in mass, and consists of cylindrical branches too small to be examined without a lens. With a little magnification, however, the cross banding of axes and branches is evident, and a slight constriction at each such joint.

One of our interesting ceramiums is *C. codicola* which lives exclusively on *Codium* and has penetrating rhizoids with bulbous tips that fasten it between the host utricles. *Ceramium caudatum* (fig. 40) is representative of several delicate epiphytic forms.

Ceramium is one of the very old algal genera, established in 1797. At that time it contained many of the finely filamentous marine algae, but has been progressively restricted until now it represents a very precisely defined group.

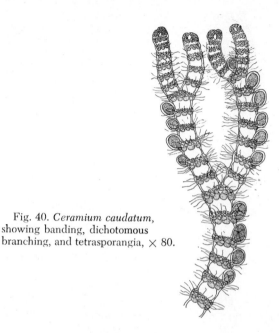

Fig. 40. *Ceramium caudatum,* showing banding, dichotomous branching, and tetrasporangia, × 80.

Centroceras (horns around a center)

There is one widespread species of this genus, *C. clavulatum,* originally described from Peru, but found throughout the temperate and tropical Pacific. We encounter it commonly on intertidal rocks as dull reddish tufts and mats. Although very delicate and filamentous, much like *Ceramium,* and seldom more than 2 inches tall, it is somewhat harsh to the touch. The cylindrical axes are regularly dichotomous and strongly incurved at the tips. They are minutely segmented and each segment has a whorl of projecting spines which are clearly visible with a lens (fig. 41). These provide the rough texture. The plant tends to fragment at the joints when it dies or is preserved.

Fig. 41. *Centroceras clavulatum,*
showing whorls of minute
spines at the tip of each
branch segment, × 100.

Spermothamnion (seed on little shrub)

Beneath the protective cover of surf grass and sometimes also on the sides and bottoms of tide pools one
observes what appears like fine pink hair an inch or
two long. This may be dense enough to form pink
patches or tufts, or may be scattered among other
small algae. These are the filaments of *Spermothamnion snyderae,* which consists of a single branched row
of elongate cells. It is distinctive in bearing asexual
spores in polysporangia (fig. 42).

This is one of the plants cultivated by the remark-
able nest-building ocean goldfish, the Garibaldi. Off
La Jolla and Point Loma this fish has been observed
to trim and cultivate certain algae to form small turf-
like patches on which the eggs are laid. *Spermotham-
nium snyderae* is one of the favored species, but another, *Murrayellopsis dawsonii,* is so exclusively a nest
alga that it has never been found anywhere except
under the care of the Garibaldi.

Polysiphonia (many tubes)

Polysiphonia is one of the familiar names among
marine algae, for these plants have long been used in
high-school and university biology classes as examples

of the Rhodophyta. This has been so not only because they are common and widely available for instructive microscopic examination, but because *Polysiphonia* was the first red alga in which the life history was conclusively worked out half a century ago.

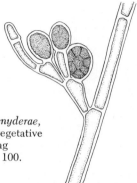

Fig. 42. *Spermothamnion snyderae,* showing elongate cells of a vegetative filament and a branch bearing developing polysporangia, × 100.

Its name refers to the multiple, often elongate and tube-like cells (pericentral cells) arranged in a cylinder around a central axial cell and, all being the same length, forming a series of "polysiphonous" segments.

We have a number of species of *Polysiphonia* of which a few, such as the tufted intertidal *P. paniculata* and the epiphytic *P. hendryi* (fig. 43), are common. The plants are usually small, mostly less than 3 inches tall, very dark reddish to almost black in mass. The tips of the branches are almost always provided with tufts of fine, colorless hairs. Although some of the larger polysiphonias can be recognized by the use of a hand lens to detect the tiers of pericentral cells and terminal hair tufts, a compound microscope is needed for specific identification.

[69]

Fig. 43. *Polysiphonia hendryi,* showing pericentral cells, terminal hairs, and male reproductive structures, × 100.

Pterosiphonia (wing tube)

This is another delicate form closely related to *Polysiphonia* but more readily identified. The commonest species, *P. dendroidea,* is a tufted intertidal, rock-inhabiting form. It is deep, dull red to almost blackish, 1–3 inches long and consists of distichous, pinnate branchlets on a flattened axis. The individual main axes look like minute feathers (fig. 44). The structure of pericentral cells is comparable with *Polysiphonia. P. baileyi* is a larger, black, coarse form to 6 inches tall with more widely spaced and less delicate pinnae.

Nienburgia (after German phycologist Nienburg)

Nienburgia andersoniana is one of our interesting representatives of the algal family Delesseriaceae which contains some of the most colorful and attractive of the membranous algae. This one consists of narrow, branched blades with a midrib in lower parts and with conspicuously toothed margins (pl. 3). It varies considerably in width and stature, up to a foot tall in sublittoral areas. We usually find smaller plants in shaded crannies and rock clefts, often growing with *Rhodymenia*. It is sometimes protected by hanks of sea-grass leaves.

A majority of the Delesseriaceae are plants of deeper waters and some extend to extraordinary depths of 200–300 feet. Many are characterized by intricate vein patterns and some, in this respect, closely resemble the leaves of higher plants.

Polyneura (many veins)

This is a brightly colored red alga of the sublittoral zone in southern California. It occurs down to depths of 30 to 40 feet and may best be collected from drift after storms. The anastomosing veins of the broad, membranous blades are unique among southern California seaweeds and make it easy to identify. The only species is *P. latissima* (pl. 4) which ranges from Can-

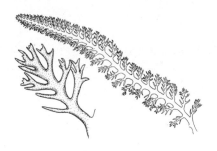

Fig. 44. *Pterosiphonia dendroidea*, showing one of the feather-like branches, × 3.5, and a detail of one of its lateral branchlets, × 35.

ada to Mexico. The plants are delicate and often are found in tattered, lacerated condition, but occasionally perfect examples up to a foot tall may be collected, and these make admirable mounted specimens. The reproductive bodies are scattered over the surfaces of the blades.

Anisocladella (unequal small branches)

Another of the delicate, membranous red algae of the surf-grass association is *Anisocladella pacifica* (fig. 45), a tiny plant only 1–2 inches tall, but of easy recognition. It may be found on most lower littoral reefs where sand patches are lodged around the roots of *Phyllospadix*. By turning back the surf grass, these little pink blades are revealed growing in the sandy turf. They are usually simple, with a midrib and distinctly toothed margins. They suggest a diminutive, unbranched *Nienburgia*.

Cryptopleura (hidden ribs)

Three of the common species of this genus may be found intertidally in southern California, two of them epiphytic. These plants are membranous forms with

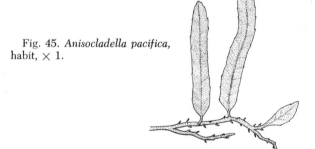

Fig. 45. *Anisocladella pacifica,* habit, × 1.

Fig. 46. *Cryptopleura violacea,* upper portion showing very delicate nerves, lateral fertile bladelets, and elongate intramarginal tetrasporangial sori, × 0.9.

ligulate blades bearing heavy midribs below and microscopic veins above. Well-developed plants are often characterized by blade margins provided with ruffles and (or) with small fertile bladelets. C. *violacea* is a large, usually saxicolous species 4–8 inches tall, of purplish color, with only a few marginal proliferous outgrowths, but with elongate tetrasporangial sori borne within the blade margins (fig. 46). *C. crispa* and *C. corallinara* are epiphytic species, the former on various coarse fleshy algae and 1–4 inches long with prominently ruffled margins. The latter is a minute, prostrate species usually attached to jointed coralline algae in accord with its name, but also found on fleshy forms such as the *Gelidium* in plate 7. All are lower-littoral, usually tide-pool inhabitants.

Fig. 47. *Laurencia spectabilis* var. *diegoensis,* small plant, × 1.

Acrosorium (summit sorus)

We have the single species *Acrosorium uncinatum* which is a warm-temperate plant that does not occur north of Santa Barbara. It is a curious plant, quite strictly epiphytic and seemingly adapted to distribute and reproduce itself vegetatively by manner of its small, hooked branches which cause it to become entangled and attached to varous slender, branched algae (pl. 2). Although in Atlantic and Mediterranean regions it goes through a regular life cycle, in the Pacific it rarely shows anything but vegetative reproduction. The red color, narrow, branched, membranous blades, and frequent hooked branches distinguish it.

Laurencia (after French naturalist de la Laurencie)

Most algae are recognized by their structural and morphological characters. A few have distinctive textures. This one is identifiable by smell. Unfortunately, the peculiar acrid odor is difficult to describe, and it must be learned before the plants can be recognized in the dark.

Laurencia is a genus of variable morphology. We have common examples both of cylindrical and flattened forms. They are frequently abundant in the middle and lower littoral. *L. pacifica* is perhaps the commonest—a bushy, dark purplish, fleshy plant several inches tall covered with very short, stubby branchlets which give it a papillate appearance (fig. 48). *L. subopposita* is a more openly branched form distinctive in the presence of hooked or entwining branches. *L. spectabilis* var. *diegoensis* is a pinnate, flattened species of very different habit (fig. 47). All of these, however, have a characteristic minute indentation or pit at the tip of each branch, and this sunken growing point bears a tuft of microscopic hairs. All are fleshy in consistency and composed of large, parenchymatous cells in cross section. (See *Erythrocystis*.)

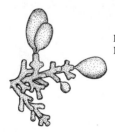

Fig. 48. *Erythrocystis saccata,* parasitic in the apical branch pits of *Laurencia pacifica,* × 1.5.

Erythrocystis (red bladder)

One of the best clues to the identification of *Laurencia*, especially *L. pacifica*, is the presence of a small, reddish-purple, bulbous, parasitic plant which grows from the apical pit of some of the branches (fig. 48). This parasitic species (*E. saccata*) is usually about a quarter inch high, but may be double that size. It is usually of simple, saccate shape, but there may be several plants borne in one pit. This is one of the few kinds of red-algal parasites which are pigmented (see *Janczewskia*).

Chondria (cartilage)

Chondria californica is a distinctive member of this genus which may often be conspicuous in tide pools on sunny days because of a striking blue iridescence. Is is a very slender, filamentous plant which characteristically has tendril-like branch tips by which it entwines the branches of other algae and fastens itself (fig. 49). Chondrias usually show a tuft of microscopic

Fig. 49. *Chondria californica*, habit on a leaf of surf grass, × 2.

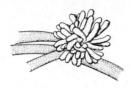

Fig. 50. *Janczewskia lappacea.* parasitic on *Chondria nidifica,* × 5.

hairs at the tip of each branch. *C. nidifica* is a larger species which is usually found in sandy places in middle littoral rocky shores where it is fastened to stones slightly embedded in sand. It is erect, cylindrical and fairly stiff. Tetrasporangial plants are most distinctive in bearing dense tufts of very short, lateral branchlets here and there on the axes. *Chondria* has a parenchymatous structure similar to *Laurencia* and *Gracilariopsis* (see *Janczewskia*).

Janczewskia (after French-Polish botanist Janczewski)

The host of one of our commonest parasitic red algae is *Chondria nidifica* which bears frequent little pale pink or whitish, burr-like growths on its axes and branches. These little burrs are fully developed plants of *Janczewskia lappacea* (fig. 50), a species restricted to the one host. Other species grow on other kinds of *Chondria* and *Laurencia*. These, like most algal parasites, are essentially without photosynthetic pigments and derive their sustenance from the host by haustorial cells which invade the host tissues. Although the vegetative plants are so reduced, the full reproductive cycle is carried out through male, female, and tetrasporangial plants as in most other Rhodophyta.

SOME REFERENCES USEFUL IN THE STUDY OF
SOUTHERN CALIFORNIA MARINE ALGAE

Dawson, E. Y. 1945. An annotated list of marine algae and marine grasses of San Diego County, Calif. San Diego Soc. Nat. Hist., Occ. Pap. (7): 1-87.

_____1953-63. Marine Red Algae of Pacific Mexico, 1-2. A. Hancock Pac. Exped. 17: 1-398, 44 pls. (1953-54); 3-4 (5 by G. J. Hollenberg), Pacific Nat. 2: 1-125, 189-375, 120 pls. (1960-61); 6, Nova Hedwigia 5: 437-476, 18 pls. (1962); 7, A. Hancock Pac. Exped. 26: 1-207, 50 pls. (1962); 8, Nova Hedwigia 6: 401-481, 45 pls. (1963). (This series includes nearly all the southern California members of this red-algal group, since they also occur in adjoining Baja California.)

_____1956. How to Know the Seaweeds. 197 pp., 259 figs. Wm. C. Brown Co., Dubuque, Iowa.

_____1959. A primary report on the benthic marine flora of southern California. pp. 109-264, In: Oceanographic Survey of the Continental Shelf area of southern California. Publ. no. 2, State [California] Water Pollution Control Board. Multilith, 560 pp. Sacramento.

Dawson, E. Y., M. Neushul, and W. D. Wildman. 1960. Seaweeds associated with kelp beds along southern California and northwestern Mexico. Pacific Nat. 1(14): 1-81, 43 pls.

Setchell, W. A. and N. L. Gardner. 1920-25. The marine algae of the Pacific Coast of North America. Pt. 2, Chlorophyceae; Pt. 3, Melanophyceae. Univ. of Calif. Publ. Bot. 8: 139-898, 95 pls.

Smith, G. M. 1944. Marine algae of the Monterey Peninsula, California, ix + 622 pp., 98 pls. Stanford Univ. Press. (This includes a large proportion of southern California species whose distributions extend north of Point Conception.)

THE SEA GRASSES

Although the vast majority of seashore plants are algae, there are many coastal localities at which one will find at least one kind of flowering plant growing under strictly marine conditions in intertidal waters or below. Sometimes these sea grasses may be so abundant as to form extensive beds on sand, mud, or rocks to the virtual exclusion of other kinds of plants. Inasmuch as only three kinds of sea grasses occur in southern California, a key to them is unnecessary and they may be identified by the illustrations and notes that follow.

Zostera (a girdle or band) Eel Grass

The true Eel Grass, *Zostera marina*, is a plant of quiet waters. It commonly lives on tidal mud flats and in bays and estuaries from low tide level down to twenty feet or more. The illustrations under figure 51 show three variants of eel grass of which those on the left represent narrow-leaved forms characteristic of sheltered bays and salt marshes, such as those near Seal Beach. The large, broad-leaf form shown on the right is known as var. *latifolia* and occurs on sheltered sandy bottom along the open coast, such as at La Jolla Bay. Fragments of these plants are commonly cast up on sandy beaches.

The flowers and fruits of eel grass are rather obscure. Part of a fertile stem is shown in figure 51, and two developing seeds are visible where the enveloping spathe does not completely cover them.

Because eel grass is an important food plant of certain birds and of many marine animals, it received a great deal of attention some years ago following its almost complete disappearance from the Atlantic Coast in 1931-1932. The significance of this destructive "wasting disease" of *Zostera* led to much research

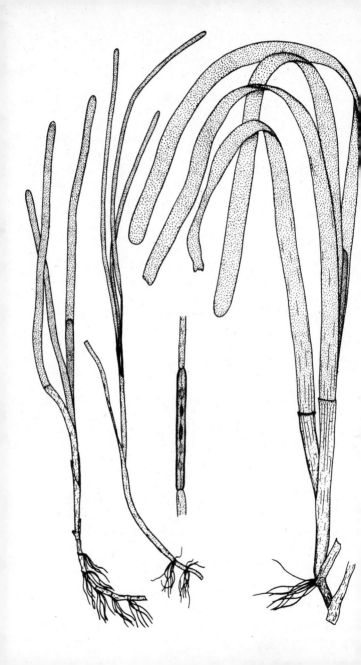

toward determining its cause, but this never was convincingly accomplished. It took fifteen years for the eel grass to return to normal growth, and there has not since been any so serious a decline.

Phyllospadix (leaf inflorescence) Surf Grass

Two species of Surf Grass occur widely along the Pacific Coast. Unlike *Zostera*, these plants normally grow in rocky places on surfy shores, from intertidal levels down to as much as 50 feet. *P. torreyi* (fig. 52) has narrow, compressed, somewhat wiry leaves and long flowering stems bearing several spadices as shown in the figure. *P. scouleri* has thinner, shorter leaves and short, basal flowering stems bearing only one or two spadices. It is especially abundant intertidally in southern California, forming extensive emerald green masses on rocky reefs near mean low tide line (pl. 2). Both of these plants are commonly mistaken by the layman for eel grass.

The seaweed collector should not overlook the importance of surf grass as a habitat for various kinds of algae. Not only do epiphytic species occur regularly on it (*Melobesia*; *Smithora*) but others are hidden beneath the protecting layer of leaves. If one simply spreads and opens up the mantle of leaves to reveal the inhabitants under them, he will find many species otherwise passed over unseen.

COASTAL SALT-MARSH VEGETATION

Apart from the strictly marine plants, which are those regularly and completely submerged by the sea water, are those seashore plants referred to as halophytes, or salt plants, which live in marine marshes where they are only partially or occasionally inundated by the sea. These are flowering plants adapted

Fig. 51. *Zostera marina,* showing three leaf forms, × 0.5, and part of a fertile stem, × 1.

Fig. 52. *Phyllospadix torreyi*, showing flowering and fruiting stems, × 0.5.

to growth in salty soil. We have a number of interesting forms along southern California in the marshes adjoining San Diego Bay, Torrey Pines State Park, Newport Bay, Seal Beach, Port Hueneme, Carpinteria, Goleta, etc. A few will be mentioned below.

Salicornia (salt horn) Pickle Weed; Glasswort

The most conspicuous of our common halophytes is *Salicornia* which is impressionable because of its peculiar succulent, jointed stems. Both annual and perennial species occur, but they are similar in appearance and rather difficult to identify specifically because of their exceedingly obscure flowers. S. *virginica* is our abundant perennial species (fig. 53). S. *bigelovii* is the commonest annual one.

Salicornia has had a long tradition of utilization in Europe as a fresh vegetable or as a pickle plant. So palatable are some of the species that in certain of

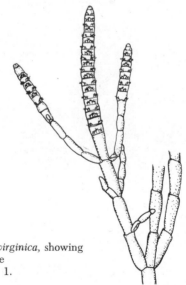

Fig. 53. *Salicornia virginica,* showing upper part of a mature plant in full flower, × 1.

the older horticultural works it was recommended that they be cultivated as a vegetable by imitating a portion of a salt marsh. Due to their high yield of soda, several species were formerly used in the making of glass and soap, the ashes of the Glasswort being known in the trade as barilla.

Distichlis (two-ranked) Salt Grass

The commonest halophytic grass along salt marshes and sandy flats of southern California is *Distichlis spicata* (fig. 54). Salt Grass is a perennial plant consisting of extensively creeping, scaly rhizomes from which stiff, harsh, and somewhat spiny leaves arise to form dense colonies. Barefoot beach-goers remember the plant well after having a stickery experience of walking on it. It tends to grow at the margins of marshes or above normal high tide line on the shore where only unusually high water may cover it. The plants are ordinarily low and spreading, 3 to 4 inches tall, but may sometimes bunch up to a foot high.

Fig. 54. *Distichlis spicata*, habit, × 0.4.

Fig. 55. *Spartina foliosa,* part of an axis with leaves, × 0.5.

Spartina (from Greek, a cord) Cord Grass

The stout, bushy, coarse grass of our salt marshes, with leaves up to half an inch broad at the base, is the California Cord Grass, *Spartina foliosa* (fig. 55). This is a plant one to three feet high, of marsh waterways in which the tide inundates it often to half or more its stature. Thus, at high water *Spartina* stands partially submerged like rice in a paddy. The leafy stems arise from extensive creeping rhizomes buried in the salty mud. The inflorescences are dense, spikelike structures 6 to 8 inches long.

Frankenia (after Swedish botanist Johann Franke, 1590-1661)

The only abundant plant of our salt marshes that bears noticeable flowers is *Frankenia grandiflora* (fig. 56), but even these "grand" pink flowers are only ⅝ of an inch across. When in full bloom, however, they are attractive and lend a modicum of bright color to the varied shades of green on the marsh. *Frankenia* is a low bush 4 to 16 inches tall with its short, narrow leaves in groups. This plant, like *Distichlis*, also inhabits the salt marsh margins where the soil is infrequently covered with salt water.

Suaeda (Arabic name) Sea Blite

Our common marsh *Suaeda* in southern California is *S. californica* (fig. 57) which is a fleshy, dull grey, decumbent to semi-erect bush 3 feet or more wide and up to 1–3 feet tall. The leaves are simple and linear, about half an inch long and usually densely clothed with microscopic, downy hairs. The flowers are small, clustered, and obscure, without any colored petals.

Several other species of *Suaeda* occur in California marshes, but most inhabit inland alkaline flats.

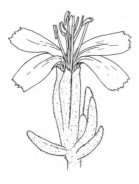

Fig. 56. *Frankenia grandiflora*: flower, × 4; habit, × 0.4.

Fig. 57. *Suaeda californica*, habit,
× 0.5; a flower, × 3.5.

COASTAL STRAND VEGETATION

The student of seashore plants cannot help but notice on his visits to the beaches and reefs for collection of algae that there are a number of plants peculiar to the slightly elevated terrestrial margins of the sea. This region of the shore, known as the coastal strand, includes environments not generally subject to inundation by seawater, as are the marine areas, proper, and the marshes, but nonetheless influenced by the adjoining sea by manner of salt spray, mist, fog, blowing and drifting sand, etc. A number of the plants there are especially adapted to life in seaside sand dunes or in the uppermost reaches of sand beaches. Several of the common and conspicuous plants of the coastal strand are pointed out and depicted below.

Abronia (graceful) Sand Verbena

Perhaps the most colorful of the dune plants are the sand verbenas of which we have three common kinds: the crimson-flowered *A. maritima* (from Point Conception southward), the rose-flowered *A. umbellata* (from Los Angeles County northward), and the yellow-flowered *A. latifolia* (from Santa Barbara County northward) (fig. 58). These are all perennial, prostrate herbs with opposite leaves and rather thick, succulent stems. The roots are usually stout and fleshy, deeply embedded in the sand. The most characteristic feature of the herbiage is its covering with minute glandular hairs which exude a sticky material to which grains of sand adhere. Thus, the plants appear as if sprinkled with sand, but one finds that the sand does

Fig. 58. *Abronia maritima*, habit, × 0.5; flower and fruit.

Fig. 59. *Oenothera cheiranthifolia*, habit, × 0.5; mature fruit, × 1.

not shake off. The flowers are fragrant and are borne in dense clusters. The flowering season is long, extending from February to October or November.

Oenothera (Wine scenting) Evening Primrose)

The evening primrose of the southern California coastal strand is the yellow-flowered *O. cheiranthifolia*. This is a plant of silvery pubescent foliage which consists of a basal rosette of thick, oblanceolate leaves from which several prostrate or decumbent stems radiate for 4 to 20 inches. The flowers are quite large, with bright yellow petals up to an inch long, sometimes with reddish spots. They appear in spring and continue throughout the summer. The fruiting capsules become peculiarly coiled at maturity (fig. 59).

Atriplex (ancient Latin name) Salt Bush

The salt bushes are characteristic plants of alkaline sinks, dry lakes, and saline areas throughout the West. Several species occur in our coastal salt marshes and we have others along the southern California sea

Fig. 60. *Atriplex leucophylla*, habit, × 0.5; fruit, × 3.

beaches and coastal strand. A common one is *A. leuco-phylla* (fig. 60). Some of the inland salt bushes and weedy forms that appear in waste places are natural-ized from Eurasia and from Australia.

These are mostly dull-looking shrubs of grayish or whitish color. They bear separate male and female flowers which are obscure, small structures without colored parts. There is nothing glamorous or striking about the salt bushes, but they are often a prevalent component of the seashore vegetation and should be recognized for their importance in this narrowly restricted terrestrial environment which adjoins the marine environment.

Mesembryanthemum (midday flower) Ice Plant

This is a very large genus of succulent plants native to southern hemisphere regions, particularly South Africa, where hundreds of species provide some of the most colorful natural ground covers in the world. Because of their abundant flowers, often of striking

[90]

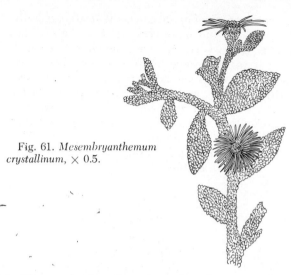

Fig. 61. *Mesembryanthemum crystallinum*, × 0.5.

brilliance, the ice plants have long been popular garden plants in the warm, coastal regions of California. They have also been used widely as sand-stabilizing and erosion-control plants wherever a drought resistant succulent can be used. From these plantings the ice plants have escaped and become naturalized along the southern California shore. Several of them are especially well adapted to compete with the vegetation of the coastal strand, so that we find them frequently spreading over upper beach sands, trailing over bluffs and covering soils just above high tide line.

The true Ice Plant is *Mesembryanthemum crystallinum* (fig. 61), so called because of its very large vesicular cells covering the surface of stems and leaves and giving it the sparkling appearance of being adorned with globules of ice. It is an annual plant with broad, ovate leaves which are green and very succulent in spring. In summer the older plants become reddish and the leaves reduced. The flowers are white or pinkish and not especially striking.

The more conspicuous succulents that are generally called ice plants, but more correctly Sea Fig or Hottentot Fig, are two species with elongate, succulent leaves of triangular shape in cross section. These are the creeping, deep green, fleshy plants so widely used as roadside binders and as erosion-control plants on dry slopes. We have a red-flowered one (*M. chilense*) native of South America, and a yellow-flowered one (*M. edule*) native of South Africa (fig. 62). The latter was traditionally a food plant of the Hottentots since the fruits are edible.

Fig. 62. *Mesembryanthemum edule*, × 0.5.

Several other species have become naturalized on sea bluffs and low ground along the shore. Although all have succulent leaves, the leaves of different species are unlike in form and appearance. The flowers, however, whether white, rose, purple, or yellow are all similar in their wheel-like shape, numerous, slender petals and abundant stamens.

Fig. 63. *Haplopappus ericoides,* habit, × 1.

Haplopappus (simple pappus) Mock Heather

Haplopappus ericoides is one of our small shrubby composites characteristically inhabiting coastal sand dunes. It is a compact, somewhat resinous, heather-like shrub 1–3 feet high with many erect branchlets bearing numerous slender, subterete leaves ½ inch long or less (fig. 63). The small yellow flower heads are produced abundantly during late summer (Aug.–Sept.) and are followed by ripe seed heads with white pappus bristles. These plants may be observed along much of the coast from Los Angeles County north. They are especially prevalent along the El Segundo dunes, in the Point Dume area and southwest of Ventura.

Fig. 64. *Convolvulus soldanella*, habit, × 0.3.

Convolvulus (to entwine) Beach Morning Glory

The morning glory of our beaches *(Convolvulus soldanella)* is another of our naturalized plants from the Old World. This pinkish or purplish-flowered one blooms from April to August along the coastal strand, living perennially from deep-seated rootstocks and producing fleshy, prostrate stems ½ to 1½ feet long from the root crown (fig. 64). The leaves are thick and somewhat fleshy. Not only do we find it along the California coast, but it extends north to Washington and occurs also in South America and on many other Pacific sea shores.

SOME REFERENCES TO SOUTHERN CALIFORNIA SEASHORE
PLANTS OTHER THAN MARINE ALGAE

Dawson, E. Y. 1945. An annotated list of marine algae and marine grasses of San Diego County, Calif. San Diego Soc. Nat. Hist., Occ. Papers (7): 1-87.

_____1956. How to know the seaweeds. 197 pp., 259 figs. Wm. C. Brown Co., Dubuque.

Mason, H. L. 1957. A flora of the marshes of California. 878 pp., 367 figs. Univ. of California Press.

Munz, P. A. 1963. A California flora. 1681 pp., 134 figs. Univ. of California Press.

_____1965. Shore wildflowers of California, Oregon, and Washington, 124 pp., 273 figs. Univ. of California Press.

GLOSSARY

agarphyte: an alga from which agar can be obtained.

alternation of generations: the reproduction of organisms that do not necessarily or precisely resemble the parent, but the grandparent; applied especially to the regular succession of gametophyte and sporophyte phases.

anastomosing: joined or united like the parts of a network.

apical cell: a single cell at the apex of a thallus or its branch from which growth emanates.

articulated coralline: a calcareous alga of the family Corallinaceae in which the stony segments are separated by minute uncalcified, flexible joints.

attenuate: gradually narrowed toward the apex.

axial filament: a cellular filament or strand running in the morphological axis of a thallus.

blade: the more or less broad, flattened, foliose part of an erect alga.

carpospore: a kind of spore in the red algae developing usually within a crystocarp which arises after sexual fusion on the female gametophyte plant.

coenocyte: a term traditionally applied to an alga with multinucleate cell or cells.

compressed: somewhat flattened so that the cross section is elliptical.

conceptacle: a cavity opening to the thallus surface and containing reproductive organs.

corymbose: shaped like a corymb in which the branches form a somewhat flat-topped cluster.

crustose: in the form of a crust.

cystocarp: the "fruit" resulting from fertilization in Rhodophyta, usually bearing carpospores within a pericarp.

decumbent: lying down, but with the tip ascending.

determinate: having limited growth.

diatomite: a soft, chalk-like sedimentary rock composed of fossil diatoms.

dichotomous: forked.

digitate: resembling the fingers of a hand.

discoid: resembling a disc.

distichous: in two ranks.

divaricate: diverging widely.

emergent: protruding prominently.

epiphyte: a plant that grows on another plant.

gametophyte: a plant that produces gametes.

geniculate: bent or shaped like the limbs at a flexed elbow or knee.

habit: the gross aspect of a plant.

haptera: basal outgrowths that form part of a holdfast.

haustorial: pertaining to the appendages of parasitic plants which enter the host and absorb nutriment.

holdfast: the basal attachment organ of an alga.

hygroscopic: readily absorbing and retaining moisture.

inflorescence: an aggregation of flowers clustered together in a particular manner.

linear: long and narrow.

medulla: the central or median tissue region of a thallus.

meristem: the point or region from which active growth takes place.

oblanceolate: inversely lance-shaped.

obligate epiphyte: living in such close relationship on another plant that no alternate habitat is acceptable.

papilla: a small superficial protuberance.

pappus: a crown of bristles at the summit of the seed in Compositae.

parenchymatous: resembling parenchyma; consisting of comparatively thin-walled cells of more or less isodiametrical form.

pedicellate: provided with a stalk or pedicel.

pericentral cell: one of a ring of cells cut off from and surrounding a central (axial) cell in the red algae.

phycocolloid: a colloidal substance obtained from seaweeds.

phycologist: one who studies algae.

phylum: one of the largest divisions or categories of the plant or animal kingdoms by which organisms are classified.

pinnae: the individual divisions or parts of a pinnate axis.

pinnate: having the divisions arranged on each side of a common rachis; feather-like.

polysporangia: sporangia in the red algae in which many spores are produced in a group.

polystichous: in several to many ranks.

proliferous: showing the development of regenerative offshoots, ordinarily in the sense of unusual position or abundance.

pubescent: covered with soft, short hairs; downy.

recurved: curved back or down.

rhizoid: a slender, root-like attachment filament consisting of a single cell or of a row of cells.

rhizome: a rootstock or dorsiventral stem, usually prostrate, producing roots as well as stems or leaves.

saccate: in the form of a sack.

saxicolous: growing on rocks.

secund: arranged along one side of an axis.

segment: one of the divisions of a jointed, segmented, or divided thallus.

septate: provided with partitions or walls.

simple: unbranched.

sorus (sori): a group or cluster of reproductive organs.

spadix (spadices): a kind of flower spike with a fleshy axis.

spathe: a large bract enclosing a flower cluster (spadix).

spermatium: a non-motile male gamete in the red algae.

spinulose: provided with diminutive spines.

sporophyte: a plant that produces spores, generally the generation alternating with the gametophyte.

stipe: the stem-like, usually basal part of a thallus.

subterete: somewhat or almost cylindrical.

sympodial: a mode of development in which the apparent main axis is not developed by continuous terminal growth, but is made up of successive secondary axes, each representing a branch.

tetraspore: a spore formed in a group of four in a tetrasporangium.

thallus: the whole plant body of an alga.

undulate: wavy.

utricles: vesicle-like cells or coenocytic structures forming a superficial tissue as in *Codium*.

verticillate: arising in a whorl from a single point of attachment.

whorl: a ring of branches or other parts arising from a single position on an axis; verticil.

zoospore: a motile spore with one or more flagella or cilia by the vibration of which it swims.